MAN *of* LIGHT

MAN

of

LIGHT

*The Extraordinary Healing Life
of Mauricio Panisset*

Kimberly Panisset Curcio

SelectBooks

This edition published by SelectBooks, Inc. For information address
SelectBooks, Inc., New York, New York.

First Edition

ISBN 1-59079-013-8

Library of Congress Cataloging-in-Publication Data
Curcio, Kimberly P.
Man of Light–1st ed.

Manufactured in the United States of America

10 9 8 7 6 5 4 3 2 1

This book is dedicated to Mauricio Panisset,
the Man of Light.
Mauricio, you add light to many lives,
all to the glory of God.
Thank you for loving me.

Acknowledgments

I would like to acknowledge Marshall Smith for his love, support, and assistance with this book. I could not have remembered all the details about Mauricio without him. Marshall, even though you are my stepfather, you have always treated me as your own. Thank you for always being there for me. You touched all of our lives when you married my mom. You have been a consistent source of love and inspiration to me as well as to so many others. When you and Patricia dropped everything to come to come to my aid in Brazil, it was your selflessness and unconditional love that enabled me to carry on. You are and always have been a true example of wisdom. I cherish our experience together and the knowledge you have shared with me.

To my mother Patricia Hayes, who is my rock, my true friend, and my great teacher in so many ways. Her love for me has been constant and her faith in me has never wavered. Patricia, it was your confidence in me and your inspiration that helped give me the courage to follow my own true path. Both you and Dad taught me what it means to love unconditionally, and it is love that has always guided me. Your unwavering commitment to God's service has brought a much greater light into our world.

A special thanks to my dearest friend Linda Bowman, who gave of herself so freely in so many ways to help make this book a reality. Her encouragement and perseverance helped make my dream come true. She worked with me many hours, typing into the wee hours of the morning, month after month. We shared many memories and many tears recalling my life with Mauricio. Thank you Linda for being a source of inspiration to me and for all that you have done. You are, and always will be the truest of friends. And thanks also go to you Lee Bowman, for sharing your wife and your home. I know it wasn't easy.

I acknowledge Susan Kramer for her expertise, and for helping me to move forward with this project. Thank you Susan for bringing order, and for dedicating your time and your love in making this book a reality. I could not have done it without you. I love you and value your work more than you know.

I would also like to give thanks my dear friend Ruth de Oliviera who along with her husband Raimond, her son Alessandro, and her daughter Alessandra, assisted me greatly in finding and translating information about Mauricio and Brazil.

To my right arm and special assistant Dorothy Adams, without whom I would be lost. Thank you Dorothy, for your tireless devotion and dedication. You have always done all that you have been asked, and I truly appreciate the love and the loyalty you have shown to me and to our family.

To my sister Kelly Hayes I give my heartfelt thanks, for her dedication to Mauricio and to me. Kelly, you are my loyal comrade and friend. Our mission together has just begun. I look forward to the future we will share.

I honor the life of my father, Harry Hayes (1934–2002), free spirit, father of six, and friend to so many. Thank you Daddy, for teaching me the difference between experiencing life and just living it. You showed me a different way, and taught me never to settle for less, and to always follow my dreams.

And last but not least, I give special thanks and my undying love to my husband and best friend Charles Curcio. Thank you Charles for finding me and for showing me that I could love again. You changed my life forever when you opened my heart and loved me. You touched my soul in places I didn't know I could feel again. You are my love and my strength, and I will cherish you always. Thank you for always being there for me, for giving yourself selflessly in any way you can to make my dreams come true. I love so much the sharing of our purpose together.

Foreword

by Dr. Wayne Dyer

Mauricio Panisset was the most unique individual I have ever met personally. He literally glowed with the high energy of love and light. When I first walked into a room with him, I immediately felt that he was radiating an extremely high energy from his body. He was gentle, exceptionally kind, and had an aura of peace that was infectious to everyone. He appeared to be ego-less, never taking any credit for his phenomenal gifts, but always attributing his light energy and healing presence to God. Upon meeting Mauricio I was immediately placed at ease and I felt as if I were in the company of someone who could actually touch my soul.

I had several actual healing experiences with Mauricio before his seemingly untimely departure, and I observed firsthand the lights emanating from his body that have been so richly described by his wife Kimberly in the pages of this book. Yet it wasn't the lights that left that lasting impression in me—I will always recall his unconditional love and his willingness to give completely of himself, so much so that he was totally drained after a session of light-giving. Moreover, he had to consume gallons of water and reclaim his expended energy with isolated rest, such was his devotion to giving and allowing God's Healing Light to work through him.

His smile was as big as the sky and his willingness to help any and all in need left me in a state of awe. The poet Rumi once said, "sell your cleverness and purchase bewilderment." I believe Mauricio Panisset was in a state of Holy Bewilderment at his enormous capacity to radiate light and healing energy, and he left me feeling the same way towards him, both in Maui and again in Georgia. I was transfixed by the enormity of this man's fine healing soul, and I am honored to say so in the opening pages of this profound book.

All Love and Light,
Wayne W. Dyer

Preface

I was born in June. My name is Marshall. When I was growing up, Papa came into our lives.

When he was little, he saw the most beautiful blue lights. These lights did no harm. He became very much in touch with this light and the light went into his body. He grew up with this light.

He married my mommy and that is how I met my papa, the light man. Now I know this light too. The light and energía heals the people. Papa had many beautiful colored lights and when Patrick, my brother, was sick, Papa would heal us. God gave a beautiful gift to Papa and he shared all with us and loved us very much.

He was hard, but even though he was hard, he was a fair man and lots of fun. He took us to Brazil and we learned lots of Portuguese. We met lots of people and many friends there. Papa taught us to play soccer and we became very good at it. We went back and forth from Brazil. I loved him very much. I loved calling Papa "the light man" and for years we had a lot of fun. Papa died of a heart attack. We went through much difficulty. I miss him, but when I see his light, I say, "The light man is coming." When we see his light, Patrick and I sometimes cry. Mommy cries the most. We are very sensitive to his light.

Papa taught us magic. He could make things disappear. He loved to play like that. Papa will be remembered by many. He touched so many people with his gifts.

—Marshall Smith, Age 9

Papa's memory lives on through all of us. I am proud to share his light with all of you. I know you will carry this light and energía in your lives too. Thank you.

—Marshall \Smith, Age 16

When I was three years old I met Papa, the Light Man. It didn't take long for Papa to win my heart. Papa and I got along really well. There is nothing I did not like about him. He was a great person as well as a great father. Papa showed me how to play soccer, and I was really good at it too. And he taught me magic. The magic he did was really cool. But most of all Papa taught me to heal. I love him. He was really great to us and Mommy. He made us feel great. He makes everybody feel great. He brought me far in life, and I know he will be with us forever, especially in my heart. I love you Papa. Thanks for everything you did.

—Patrick Smith, Age 12

Introduction

MAURICIO PANISSET was truly a man of light, a Brazilian healer gifted with rare phenomena. Bright lights could be seen flashing like lightning coming from various parts of his physical body when he performed healing work. The lights varied in color according to the needs of the people. The lights came to Mauricio when he was nine years old, and remained with him for fifty-four years until his death.

Mauricio was schooled in engineering and physics, and was a professor for thirty-seven years in the university system of Brazil. He was employed by the Brazilian Justice Ministry in Brazilia for eight years before moving to the United States. Mauricio was associated with and did healings on several Brazilian cabinet ministers as well as one Brazilian president

This is a true story. Everything you are about to read is based upon my own personal experience in the years living with and being married to Mauricio. Some of the things I relate to you may seem unlikely. Others may seem impossible. I know you will find Mauricio fascinating. His healing work inspired many people to discover that there is much more to life than suffering and struggle. He believed that God is indeed here on earth, and that he works through ordinary people like you and me.

> When you discover the light that is within you,
> You will desire to bring a greater part of your
> Spirit into matter,
> And by doing so, you bring a greater light into
> our world.

1

Out yonder there is a huge world, which exists
independent of us human beings and which
stands before us like a great, eternal riddle.

–Albert Einstein

W HEN MY SON Marshall was five years old, he came running up to me, falling all over his words as he desperately
tried to describe what he had just witnessed. He had seen
the unexplainable—bright physical lights coming directly out of a
man's body. To his young unadulterated soul, this was a wonderful
and magical event, no stranger than the sun shining in the sky. There
was no fear or questions about what he had beheld, only the wonder
of a child who has just seen and felt something marvelous. He wanted to know all about the man who possessed such magic, and how he
too could do such things. After a few moments of frustration at trying to find the words, he finally exclaimed, "You know, you know,
Mommy, The Light Man."

The memory sent chills through my body and brought me back to
the present. It was dry and breezy, just like any other typical winter
day in Brasilia. The sun's rays were beating down heavily, but that did-
n't seem to matter. Because we lived without air conditioning, we had
long ago become accustomed to the natural warm air here. The taxi
was nearing the airport, and I was looking out the window staring at,
but not seeing, the myriad of beautiful flowers along the side of the
road that adorn this unique city. Flowers are everywhere in Brasilia,
and the city's exquisite beauty usually charmed and captivated me.

You can feel the raw energy here, naturally emanating from the
ancient crystalline rocks that form the foundation of this futuristic

city. Beginning with its earliest prophecy over two centuries ago, Brasilia has been an enduring myth. In 1883 Father Guiseppe Bosco, a well known Italian Mystic, whose visions had a habit of coming true, dreamed that angels carried him into the Amazon to a spot where a new Brasilian capital would be built. A voice told Dom Bosco "...a great civilization will appear here, the Promised Land, flowing with milk and honey." The prophecy that determined Brasilia's location, a mystical site atop some of the earth's most significant crystal deposits, befits the intense spiritual nature of the Brasilians and the country's long history of supernatural and paranormal events. I witnessed many of these extraordinary events firsthand while living in Brasil. A lot of them occurred through and because of my husband.

But on this day my perception was clouded. Everything seemed so surreal. All I was feeling was the pain in my heart, and the disillusionment of my own perceived failures that were forcing me to leave the country that had become my home. In the background I could hear Marshall, now ten years old, and the more gregarious of my two sons, deep in conversation with the taxi driver. Patrick, my other son, who was only nine, was sitting quietly next to me. I wished in this moment that he were not so sensitive. I was feeling overwhelmed, and the closer we got to the airport, the heavier my heart felt the burden. Patrick had enough to worry about without sharing in my emotions, especially since he no longer remembered his native language. Suddenly I became aware of a voice outside of me, and I realized that Patrick was trying to get my attention. I looked down into his incredibly deep blue all-knowing eyes framed by the white sandy hair covering his brow. He was telling me in Portuguese that we had arrived at the airport. I could see his concern for me, and I tried to hide my emotions. Spirit had always given me the ability to face adversity, and now once again I was in the hands of fate. At least we will leave with grace, I thought. I touched Patrick's face, softly acknowledging him. I could see that he too was being brave. My heart went out to him, but I knew he would be okay.

Marshall, Patrick, and I stood on the tarmac outside, looking up at the roof where all the people stood to say goodbye to us before we actually boarded the airplane. All of our friends and many children were standing there, enthusiastically waving their last good-byes, and crying at the same time. My tears were blinding me, and I couldn't walk up the steps to the plane. Why did letting go have to be so difficult? Why did it have to feel so painful? A part of me wanted to tear out my heart and hurl it into the wind. Perhaps then my pain and longing for this life I was leaving would be over. And then I could forget. My mind was racing. But at the same time I didn't want to forget anything. Would Brasil be forgotten, distant in the corner of my mind, or would I return here one day to continue and fulfill my dreams? It seemed like only yesterday. It was hard to believe that almost a year had passed since my love left us.

I smiled, sensing that it was time to board. I took one of the longest breaths I had ever taken, and I felt an inner strength as a feeling of peace calmly washed over me. As I turned, my legs felt guided as if they didn't need any support. I was gliding on air effortlessly up the tall steps to the airplane, and before I knew what was happening, the plane was taxiing off. As I sat gazing out the window, tears again streamed uncontrollably from my eyes. I knew intuitively that I had made the right decision to leave. It was foolish of me to think that one woman could singlehandedly take on such an enormous and difficult project in a country that was not her own. I was still confused, not knowing now what my purpose was, and what the future would hold for us in our new life back in the United States.

Although I was feeling lost, it was necessary for me to maintain a sense of balance for our little family. Marshall and Patrick were really all that mattered right now, and getting us back to our home in Georgia that Mauricio and I had built together. I remembered that only six months before I couldn't even fathom the idea that I could ever live there again without him. It had been far too painful to even consider, until now.

I tried to get comfortable, since this was only the first leg of our trip, and we had a long way to go. I closed my eyes and laid back in reflection. I was standing alone in the darkness, when shadows of light began to dance and move around me. The lights got brighter and brighter, and I was soon captivated by their brilliance. And then I felt a presence, as waves of energy moved through me. I knew it was Mauricio. I felt safe and I felt loved. I became aware that my breathing was changing, and I became completely calm. The energy was so soothing and comforting that I wished I could stay like this forever. I felt assured that everything was in divine order, even though it was beyond my understanding. Time I thought, time is all I need. Only through time would these sad feelings leave, and only in time could I discover how this great love would continue to express itself here on Earth.

My mind drifted back, back into time, back to that momentous day when my mother Patricia, and my stepfather Marshall, who I call Papa, were just returning from their first spiritual journey to Brasil. I didn't know why, but I was most anxious to see them, more so than usual. I felt extremely restless, so I drove up to McCaysville, a little town in the Blue Ridge Mountains of North Georgia where they lived, and waited for them to arrive. It was only a two-hour drive from my apartment, and I felt compelled to go. I couldn't wait a moment longer. The anticipation I felt seemed a bit strange, as they were only gone for two weeks, and they traveled all the time. But I missed them so much. I was supposed to be on that trip too, but at the last minute I was unable to go. It was curious how destiny had kept me from going.

When I finally met them, Patricia and Marshall were full of energy. Their eyes glowed with a warm and gentle love. Their very presence emanated light. I was amazed at the stories they told me. Their lives had been touched very profoundly, and were changed forever because of that trip they had taken to Brasil. My Papa began to describe a man whom he and Patricia met and with whom they shared an instant connection. He was a Brasilian man named Mauricio Panisset, who possessed an extraordinary gift of healing. When Mauricio worked, actual physical lights came out of his body. I didn't totally comprehend what he was telling me, but I could feel the truth of what he was saying about this man. I was awe struck as my Papa continued, for I knew in some strange way that everything he was saying was not only the truth, but somehow I was connected to it. I didn't know how, but I was sure I would find out.

Marshall then described his first encounter with Mauricio. Mauricio was standing at the doorway of the hotel in a black leather jacket. He looked uncomfortable and he was unbearably shy. So much so, that he could hardly walk up to the group. Marshall thought, "this is him, huh?" Marshall sensed what Mauricio was going through, and his compassion went out to him. He too had grown up being shy and knew how painful it could be. As Mauricio slowly made his way over to the group, Marshall could even hear him thinking, "What am I going to do with all these people?"

During the course of that evening, Mauricio worked with the thirty people in their group. The room was dark, but lit dimly with candles. There were several healing tables lined up next to each other, covered with white sheets. The room was electric. Music, the

Kodoish Hymn, was playing softly in the background, and there was a sacred feeling here, a feeling of reverence for God, and an anticipation that something very special was about to happen.

When it was their turn, Marshall and Patricia lay on tables that were next to each other and closed their eyes. Mauricio began to speak softly in Portuguese saying, "Energia, energia, energia." With their eyes closed, they could see flashes of light moving all around them. Patricia opened her eyes for a moment only to see bright lights flashing all around and coming from Mauricio. Startled, she quickly closed them. Mauricio was moving around the table, and as he touched her on the forehead she felt intense heat traveling as a wave of energy, that moved from the top of her head all the way down to her toes. She also felt a deep feeling of peace and relaxation. As he continued to work on her, she began to see things with her eyes closed. As he spoke different words she saw different colored lights. There were images of spiritual beings coming close to her and then moving away. She felt she had known some of these spiritual beings before in the distant past and she felt totally loved. She knew she had known Mauricio before too. She heard a door close and knew Mauricio had left, but many of the spiritual beings were still there. When she finally got up she could barely walk. That night, Patricia and Marshall couldn't sleep, and they were up all night sharing their experiences with each other. Patricia remained in a state of Nirvana for three days.

Patricia's eyes spoke volumes, and I was greatly moved by her presence and the quiet peace that surrounded her. I had not seen her this way before. Marshall, who is normally quiet and reserved, could hardly contain himself, and I knew something profound had touched them both. I felt an unbelievable pull towards this Brasilian energy and at the same time it felt very uncomfortable. But I was excited and intrigued and I wanted to know more.

The connection they had made with Mauricio was immediate and powerful. To them it was a reunion with a long lost friend and cosmic brother whom they hadn't seen in a long time. They were elated, as was Mauricio, and all of them were determined to discover what this connection was. As fate would have it, Mauricio's schedule and itinerary coincided exactly with their own, and the next day they were all on their way to Sao Paulo where the tour continued. Mauricio had an appointment there to do healing work with the son of a government minister, who had been in a serious car accident, and was in critical condition. Mauricio became so enamored with Patricia and Marshall that he accompanied them on the rest of the tour, only separating from them when necessary.

However separated they were during the daytime, they always looked forward to the evenings together in his hotel room, where they could share on a more personal level. Marshall was never a big talker, nor was he really big on socializing either. But when he got together with Mauricio, it was so easy for him to open up. Their interests were similar, and in these evenings they shared many stories. They even discussed the Bible, and certain figures from the Bible. Mauricio would say, "You know him?" And Marshall would reply, "Yes, I do," and would elaborate on the subject, which always impressed Mauricio.

Every now and then, when Mauricio would get up out of his seat and go to the bathroom, light would shoot out of his lower abdominal area, out of his first chakra. This happened the first time they were together and it startled Marshall and Patricia. Not only that, but as he walked towards the bathroom, wooden crosses began falling out of the air behind him. Astonished, Marshall and Patricia picked them up, and asked, "Where did these come from? How did you do that?" Mauricio only laughed. He was relaxed and having fun. Phenomena such as materialization and light manifestation were ordinary events for him, but to Patricia and Marshall they were extraordinary, and represented a rare glimpse of the divine. Mauricio treated these things as if they were an every day occurrence, which for him they usually were.

Patricia and Marshall finally walked back to their rooms at about 4:00 am. It was a special evening they shared with this special man. As they lay their heads down to sleep, soft currents of energy continued to flow through their bodies. They felt every atom, molecule, and cell electrified and being harmonized.

When they awoke, the feeling in the air was still mystical, except that the air seemed so much fresher than the night before. Everything looked crystal clear. They were having so much fun with their new friend.

On that morning there was another surprise. On the table next to Patricia's bed were three wooden crosses that were not there when she went to bed. They were fascinated and yet puzzled. Mauricio had never been in their room, yet the crosses were there. It had been an amazing journey and continued to get more intriguing with each moment.

In Sao Paulo Mauricio accompanied them everywhere. One morning they were sitting with the tour having breakfast at the Hilton Hotel. A Brasilian woman in the group who hadn't spoken much was telling Mauricio about her 23-year-old daughter who had recently died. She was crying as she talked. She told everyone that she and her daughter had moved from Brasil to California years ago and that her daughter had been diagnosed with cancer. Their lives had been torn apart. Everyone at the table could feel her pain, and most had tears in their eyes as she told the story of her daughter's decline. She finally decided to bring her daughter home to Brasil to see if the Brasilian healers could help her. Every healer they visited told her the same thing, "Take your daughter home; I can't help her." The woman was really sobbing now. Mauricio, who had been listening intently like everyone else, suddenly reached over and touched the woman's neck and pulled out a cross, a small, unique filigree cross with a lot of circles on it. When Mauricio handed it to her, she burst out crying uncontrollably. "Oh, my God, oh, my God, that's the cross my daughter was cremated with." The rest of the group sat frozen, staring in disbelief. When the woman could finally talk she told everyone the cross in her hand, the one Mauricio pulled from her neck, was the cross her daughter had worn when she was cremated a short time ago. No one said a word.

The woman looked into Mauricio's eyes, searching for an answer. Then a deep sense of peace came over her. Mauricio gently told her that her daughter had sent the cross to her to say that she was okay and not to grieve anymore, that she was still alive and well and that she loved her. The mother told Mauricio that he was an angel, and that this miracle is why she felt so compelled to come on this healing journey. Mauricio leaned over and kissed her on the cheek, and just as it had mysteriously begun, the whole experience was over. Everyone got on the tour bus as usual, but no one would be the same after that morning. Mauricio later told Patricia and Marshall that he had been drawn into the woman's energy as she was telling her story. It wasn't his nature to move into people's energy unless there was a great need. He felt the need for healing and he responded to it.

2

To dream anything that you want to dream—
that is the beauty of the human mind. To do
anything you want to do—that is the strength
of the human will. To trust yourself to test
your limits—that is the courage to succeed.

–Bernard Edmonds

BRASIL IS AN enchanting land. Even though it is a Catholic country, there exists a blend of religion and spiritualism that is unique in all the world. Phenomena and spiritual healing are commonplace, and it is not unusual for someone to seek out a spiritual healer just like someone in America might seek out a medical specialist. There are many spiritual mediums in Brasil, each with their own style and system. The country itself radiates a strong vital energy, which has always been conducive to psychic phenomena and spiritual healing. Brasil has a way of opening your eyes to possibilities beyond human comprehension.

On their continuing journey in Brasil, Patricia and Marshall met another unusual channel whose name was Luis Gasparatto. Gasparatto is a psychotherapist who has a clinic in Sao Paulo. He is an extraordinary man, a spiritual medium that channels the artwork of great artists who have passed away. As the group watched him work, Patricia and Marshall were sitting directly in front of him, about six feet away. He put on a blindfold, and stood in front of a canvas as he painted a 2 x 3 foot work of art in just two minutes. When he was finished, he took off the blindfold, looked upon his work, and smiled simply. It was an incredible painting that looked exactly like the original Degas masterpiece. No one would believe it unless he or she saw it. Even I had trouble as I listened to their story. Gasparatto told the group that when this phenomenon first began years earlier, he felt that he was doing it himself, and that it wasn't being channeled at all. But just as his arrogance set in, the channeling stopped, and he was unable to paint for a long time.

Gasparatto then sat back on a chair with the canvas in front of him. He was blindfolded once again. Only this time he picked up the paintbrush with his toes. The movements were fast and furious as he dipped his brush first in one color, and then another. In a matter of minutes he had painted a replica of one of Van Gogh's famous works. When he finished the "Van Gogh," Gasparatto went on to explain to the group that he finally realized and understood over time that the Great Masters were using his brain and motor skills to do the painting. Subsequently he had access to all of his own abilities as well as the Masters, and the creativity of the Masters could channel through him. In order to do this, one has to be spiritually aware and willing to give up control. It was only through his own experience that Gasparatto grew to understand the actual process of what was happening to him.

The first healer that Patricia and Marshall encountered on their tour was Brother Luis, who works with a spirit doctor known as Dr. Fredericks. Brother Luis was described as a rough character. When the group arrived, they were brought into his museum where there were hundreds of jars of body parts that had been removed and taken from people who had received psychic surgery from Dr. Fredericks working through Brother Luis. The group was required to view these jars, and those that didn't participate could not attend the healing. Some of our people felt queasy, but everyone complied.

On display there were also big spirit pictures of Dr. Fredericks. You could actually see his image as a cloud. The group was taken into a big assembly room for a long sermon in Portuguese, which only two of our people understood. The evening had begun well, but it soon became long and repetitive. Marshall felt that it was wearing him down. He knew he would get a healing just through surrendering to the events. He kept repeating to himself, "I've got it. I've got it." It was almost as if the good doctor were trying to wear you down, to break down your resistance and the façades, leaving you so tired that there was nothing left to do but surrender to spirit and healing.

Brother Luis' quarters were small, and it was hot. Imagine for yourself, several hundred people standing and listening for hours to a lecture in Portuguese, while awaiting their healing. Americans usually don't fare well in these circumstances, having to wait for what seemed an eternity. When they were finally ready, they divided the group, with half going one way, and the other half going another.

There were numerous healers working in this center, each in a separate room with a red light burning at each table. Only when you entered the room could you actually see the healers, who would then place their hands upon you wherever they felt the need. One healer could manifest blood, and anyone who got a healing from this particular man ended up with a big red circle of blood on his or her clothes right over their solar plexus. Since everyone was dressed in white, imagine how embarrassing it must have been for them to go back to the Sheraton with blood on their stomachs and on their clothes.

The purpose of all phenomena is for spiritual awakening. Mauricio explained that phenomena not used for this purpose are out of order. Phenomena often provided the assistance a person needed to accept his or her healing, and to believe that such things were possible. Mauricio told the group that many times people came only to see the phenomena and for no other reason. They really didn't need healing or want it. This really bothered him, and it often made him stop and wonder if he should continue. You could feel his dissatisfaction as he spoke about it in his broken English. He went on to say that others were spiritually awakened by the experience, but not enough for them to heal. He said if people just get caught up in the phenomenon they won't benefit spiritually from his work. They could say, "Wow, look at that blood on my stomach." Mauricio would respond, "Well, what did you receive?" And they would answer, "I don't know, I didn't feel anything. But I have blood on my stomach". On the other hand, a person could be so impressed and moved by faith that in an instant, they are healed.

One man who came to Delphi to visit Alex Orbito, a Filipino Psychic Surgeon, said after he experienced the surgery, "Now, I know there is a God." This was a spiritual awakening. The man knew there was something more, something greater than himself. He learned beyond a shadow of a doubt, that there is a greater power that we can draw upon, a power far greater than man that is operating within the universe.

Mauricio said that we don't have to feel that we are always victims of our own weaknesses or of the world. There is a reason why we often have to get sick before we really begin to feel better about ourselves. Sickness becomes our teacher. We learn to listen, and to be more sensitive to our needs, and to the needs of others. We must learn to love and forgive ourselves as well as others. Most of all we must live our destiny to its fullest, with the courage and trust that every single thing that occurs in one's life is significant and will hold seeds for the building of our immediate future.

Another city they visited on the tour was Salvador, a very old and mystical place, and one of the most ancient cities in Brasil. The group went there to see Franco Valdo, another spiritual medium and healer. He was very gracious and friendly, and a most practical man. Franco would pick up abandoned children throughout the City of Salvadore, and would take them to his orphanage. There he would feed them, clothe them, and educate them. He showed the group the teenagers that had been training with him for years. He also ran the most organized day care center Patricia had ever seen, which served young couples who couldn't afford babysitters. They even provided sleds with ropes on them at the center, so they could pull the children around without the fear of them falling off, sort of like Brasilian seat belts.

That evening everyone was invited for refreshments at Valdo's home. When the group walked in, Tal Shaler, a Swiss physician and friend, came over and personally introduced Patricia and Marshall. Valdo immediately said to them, "Yes, I know who you are. The spirits are here, and they congratulate you on your wonderful work, and they encourage you to continue. They want to give you a gift. They want you to have a bouquet of roses." And with that Valdo's mouth opened wide, and the fragrance of roses filled the room so strongly that everyone just stopped talking and began to look for the source of this incredible fragrance. Valdo was smiling. He was happy. That's when Marshall realized that Valdo had not been speaking English at all! However, both Patricia and Marshall understood everything that he said in perfect English, even though he spoke only Spanish. In France Valdo speaks to entire audiences in his native tongue and they understand him in French. Being an engineer, this was most impressive to my Papa. I was most envious of this experience. What an honor to be acknowledged by spirit, and to have physical confirmation supporting the work that you do. I was moved once again.

Dr. Guedes is a psychic surgeon in Sao Paulo who uses long stainless steel needles in his healing work. He is also an Umbanda Priest and a beer distributor. What is most amazing is that he penetrates all parts of the body with these needles, and there is virtually no blood and no pain. Dr. Guedes is the most balanced and earthy healer that they met in Brasil next to Mauricio. He is unique and non-pretentious, presenting everything with simplicity.

When the tour group arrived at his healing center, they were surprised to see a large open room full of people sitting in chairs facing another open area. The room was somewhat bare. To their left also facing the open area was a group of Dr. Guedes mediums, over twenty in total. They sat in prayer during the healing sessions supplying Dr. Guedes with ectoplasm. Ectoplasm is accumulated life force energy, sometimes referred to as prana, which is concentrated through the focus of the mediums to assist with the healing process. Dr. Guedes used the ectoplasm so that the patients felt no pain during the surgery, to minimize bleeding, and to accelerate the healing process. He worked in the open area with one patient at a time. He had several assistants helping the people to get to where he was working and helping them back to their chairs. Dr. Guedes used large needles, some nearly a foot long.

Patricia has never liked needles, and she spent most of the time struggling to decide if she was going to go up and experience the healing or not. She watched the eyes of the patients closely to see if they were feeling pain. If she did go, she certainly didn't want to feel any pain. Everything seemed okay to her. Dr. Guedes operated quickly and in full view of everyone present.

As Dr. Guedes worked, everyone could see clearly. They watched as he operated on a Brasilian woman, removing her cataracts. He bent down to look up into her eyes, in her case using what looked like a steak knife in his hand. He reached out and with a sharp quick movement cut something out of her eye. Then he put two patches over her eyes. And just as soon as it had begun, it was over. There was no bleeding, and no pain, and the woman never moved an inch. A young boy that was sitting next to Patricia had eye problems too. One eye had already been operated on unsuccessfully by a regular surgeon. His parents chose Dr. Guedes for the surgery of the second eye. The boy was going blind.

Patricia panicked. She knew if she were going to do it she would be next. She watched the little one closely. He was so brave. He didn't even flinch. One of the attendants came to help her up to the front. The moment of truth had arrived. She had watched for over an hour as person after person went up for healing. One woman with back problems had over ten long scary looking needles sticking out of her back at one time. They didn't look like acupuncture needles, but more like knitting needles, big knitting needles. My mom was going to see if Dr. Guedes could help her lower back and if he could relieve the pain that she felt each morning. What if he put those large needles in her? She prayed. When the man touched her arm to help her up front, she responded and automatically followed him. During her healing, she couldn't feel even one of the needles. She wouldn't have even known they were there if the rest of the group hadn't told her. Since the healing, she has never had low back problems again.

My friend Emmy Chetkin had terrible back problems for years. She and her husband Lenny were also on the tour with Patricia and Marshall. Here is Emmy's experience in her own words:

"Every morning I would open my eyes and dread the next few hours. First the laborious exit from my bed: sliding to the edge, slowly coming to a sitting position, and then standing. My bathroom was not far but the trip was halted several times by back spasms. Then slowly over the next hour or so things would loosen up and I would actually be able to go out and run a few miles! I was a faithful chiropractic patient and received wonderful care, but this one problem was stubborn and after two years I wondered if this would be a lifelong situation. Now my husband and I were sitting in a room in Sao Paolo with many others witnessing the healing power of spirit as expressed through Dr. Guedes. We had come to Brasil with our friends Patricia Hayes and Marshall Smith on a spiritual journey, which included many Brasilian healers. Our new friend Mauricio Panisset had accompanied us to the healing center of Dr. Guedes, and we were all feeling very good. Mauricio, this wonderful 'Man of Light,' felt like a forever friend, and his very presence was a blessing to us. Behind a small railing twelve mediums sat in meditative silence, while Dr. Guedes worked on patient after patient. Our group sat in respectful silence and awe as we watched. It seems difficult to understand, and if I hadn't been there I wonder if I could ever have believed what I saw that night. Dr. Guedes worked with what appeared to be long knitting needles, screwdrivers, ordinary kitchen knives, and several other implements. He would probe with these instruments into the person's body: putting them into whatever area was the source of the patient's physical problem. I saw a knitting needle go right through a young man's neck, and that man did not even move or bat an eye. I knew in that moment that I would ask for healing. As I went forward I felt no fear, only complete trust in this man who I had only met an hour before. Behind a sheet held by female assistants I removed my shirt and was told to lie face down on the table. Dr. Guedes approached the table and began to work on my spine. He inserted six of the 'knitting needles.' I actually felt the second and the sixth needle, and the feeling was one of electricity, as if a beam of electric current had entered my back. Dr. Guedes told me that when I awoke the following morning, I would leap from my bed like an eighteen year old. He spoke in Portuguese. I heard him in English. I had no doubts, and the next morning I arose from my bed totally free from any discomfort. My back was perfect. I did experience a strange phenomenon. For about one week I felt a ball of pain hovering about eighteen inches behind my back, as if it were attached to me by a wobbling energetic current. I mentioned this to Patricia, and wise woman that she is, she told me, 'Tell it you do not need it anymore.' I did, and in that moment it dispersed like the fluff of a dandelion when you blow on it at the end of summer. Never in all the years since that night have I had a recurrence of the problem in my back. Over the years I remember to send prayerful thanks to Dr. Guedes."

3

Only those who will risk going too far can
possibly find out how far one can go.

–*T. S. Eliot*

A VOICE BROUGHT me back from these musings, back to
the airplane, back to reality. Patrick was trying to get my
attention, asking why I wasn't eating. I convinced him that I
would be sure to eat something on the next leg of the trip. I was concerned about Patrick and Marshall adjusting to America, Patrick
more than Marshall, as he no longer remembered the English language. Marshall could flow back and forth. We were leaving Brasilia
to return to the Mountains of North Georgia, to a simple place, born
because of the copper and silver deposits discovered here nearly two
hundred years ago. Most of the people who live here were born here
along with their parents and their parents before them. The commu-
nity was just now beginning to grow, attracting many summer vaca-
tioners from Florida and Atlanta because of its white water rivers and
mountain top views. My heart was somewhat partial to this little
town for one reason and one reason only. This was the place where
Delphi and my life's work were located.

Patrick was only three and Marshall four when we left the U.S for
Brasil. We lived in the jungle, about three hours outside of Brasilia,
and we adapted well to this place, a place of few amenities and crea-
ture comforts. After Mauricio died, we moved to the city of Brasilia,
where we experienced a unique and cosmopolitan culture. Each of us
would have our share of challenges in the months to come.

I looked into Patrick's incredible eyes. They were consoling for
me. I wondered what destiny held in store for my sons. I recalled all

19

of the dramatic changes they had experienced. Surely they were strong, but they were just children. What were they to learn from all of this? Did they believe in love? Would they believe it could last, or would they be afraid to love for fear of losing it? After all, a child could perceive through his personal experience that just when you find love, it leaves you. But my boys were not only sensitive; they had strong spirits that were already loving. And they both had a good balance between the thinking and feeling sides of their nature. I didn't need to worry. They were in good hands. Before I knew it, I was right back in my reverie.

It was a beautiful day, bright, sunny, and radiant. We were all helping to change Patricia's and Marshall's newly built home addition into a Healing Sanctuary. Patricia and Marshall had just finished building an octagon wing, an addition to their existing home, because they wanted and needed more room. They also built a large additional room that connected the two together. They loved their new space. The octagon was two stories. The upstairs area contained their office, and downstairs their living room. The connecting room was their new bedroom. They had only lived in their new home for two months before the healing journey to Brasil.

On the plane ride home from that trip, another unbelievable experience occurred. It had been a hectic day for them, as the ending day of all tours are, and they finally made it to their flight. Shortly after takeoff, Patricia had adjusted her seat and laid back to rest. Upon closing her eyes she began to feel waves of energy moving from her heart to her head. Two of the spiritual beings, the ones she had seen and recognized during the light energization session with Mauricio, were standing in front of her. They pulsated in an even rhythm. She was seeing them with her inner vision, but saw them as clearly as if her eyes were open. The taller of the two began communicating with her. He showed her an image of their new octagon home, and told her that if she would dedicate this new building as a healing sanctuary, many spirit doctors and healers would reside there. He showed her that the downstairs area was to be a receiving room for people to wait for healing and where they would discuss their experiences afterwards. Upstairs was to be sacred space, and to be used only for healing. There would be no discussions or talking in this space. He told her that the room would be a window to the other side, and that miraculous healings would occur. There was to be a healing service held once a month, and anyone who had a need could attend. He also said healers would come as well and volunteer their services.

It was such a powerful vision. When it was over she excitedly told Marshall all about it. He too felt the intent and purpose of their new project. When they returned from Brasil, they realized they had not added on to their house at all, but had built the perfect healing sanctuary. So, back down into the other house went all of the furniture. A wall was built to separate the two buildings, and the Delphi Healing Sanctuary was born. Little did they know at the time that Mauricio would come to live at Delphi and use the sanctuary for his healing work as well. I was somewhat amused seeing my mother scurry about in a serious manner changing everything. I thought about that film I love so much, "Field of Dreams." It reminded me of the voice that whispered "Build it and they will come."

I couldn't help but repeat that phrase over and over again in my mind as we made the changes. I could also feel and I understood what inspired them to give up this new extension of their home. We were ready to go to the next level. It was time to go even higher and bring a greater dimension of that sacred energy not only into our own lives but also into the lives of others who were searching for a greater love and for healing of those things that troubled them.

As affected as Patricia and Marshall were by Mauricio, he too had been equally affected. As a token of their love and to seal their instantaneous bond, the three of them decided to share their land. Patricia and Marshall gave land at Delphi to Mauricio, and Mauricio gave part of the Enoch Foundation land, The Fundacao Enoch, outside of Brasilia to them. This was all very fascinating to me. I had so many mixed emotions I didn't understand. I had made so many changes in my life and was just settling in. Why was my tummy feeling so anxious? Why did I feel so uncomfortable at times talking about this man? Why did I feel as if I already knew him? Whatever was going on within me was beyond my comprehension. My Mom and Papa were ecstatic. Mauricio had accepted their invitation to come to Delphi. He would be in Los Angeles two months from now and would come immediately afterwards. Patricia privately selected a group of 30 for Mauricio to work with. It wasn't hard to do. Within an hour she had a wonderful group assembled.

It was a hot and muggy that August day in '89. So many things happen for me in August, including my birthday. The day had come when Mauricio was to arrive, but everything was so iffy. His work in California had been difficult, and he was tired. He wanted to go back to Brasil to rejuvenate. After speaking to him several times by phone, Patricia convinced him to come, and assured him that he would be able to restore his energy at Delphi. Just being on the white water river here had its own healing effect. Up to this point Mauricio's emotional self had been a bit unstable. He was never comfortable going to a new place for the first time, and his emotional body could sometimes carry him away. His fear of what could happen to him sometimes got the best of him, and in some ways he was afraid of people. He didn't trust many. He didn't have complete control over these lights either, and when he got excited about something, the light would shoot out of his body involuntarily. This could happen in a restaurant or on the street, anywhere, especially when he felt free and relaxed. But he was coming to Delphi and everyone was thrilled, except for me.

As we prepared for his arrival later that day, my emotions were flittering all over the place. My Mom was making an even bigger fuss. I could understand her wanting everything perfect, but did we have to clean our big 40-foot motor home and get it ready just to pick up this one man from the airport? What was wrong with the car or the van? I had not begun to grasp the significance of this man or his visit. Even though I was a little on edge, I was flowing with it all. I was looking forward to this experience despite the underlying resistance that was tugging at my heart. I was feeling somewhat free and I liked being single. It had only been a short time. My best friend Linda Bowman was there too. She was a part of the group my Mom had put together, and she was there to help. While Marshall and Patricia were headed to the Atlanta airport to pick up Mauricio, we stayed at Delphi to greet the people who were already starting to arrive. There was an excitement in the air. Everyone was upbeat and anticipating the experience.

A few of those who had come this day had also been on the tour with Patricia and Marshall, and had already experienced Mauricio's energy. Those who had not been on the tour were astounded to hear about Mauricio in greater detail. Although they hadn't even met the man yet, their hearts had already begun to flutter. They told the others that as he performed his healing "Energizations" brilliant light emerged from his body and shot out into the room. One woman said that her intuition had increased, and that it strengthened her connection to a higher wisdom. All of them spoke of a tremendous and incredible flow of love that opened their hearts. They possessed an extraordinary sense of gratitude for their experience. You could feel it when they spoke. They were inspired and awed by his beautiful gift and the possibilities it held for their own spiritual growth and development. The stories did not seem incredible to me, and I loved hearing them. I knew they were speaking the truth. I had already witnessed the dramatic effect this man had on my Mom and Papa, and soon I found myself participating in the discussion. I was talking about Mauricio as if I knew him. It felt odd at first, and I wondered how I could know such things about a man I had never met. Chills of confirmation ran through my body. I knew I was speaking the truth. How was it this man had so much power even over our group? He hadn't even arrived yet, but, as we spoke, you could feel his presence in our room creating a high and loving ambience. There was a charge and you could feel it. Something very special was about to happen.

The evening was full of energy and charged with electricity. You could smell its sweetness. How I loved the evening air, but tonight was extraordinarily different. It has always been my custom to look up to the stars and smile and say thank you to the universe. In this night I felt gratitude and appreciation for the experience that was to come. I couldn't understand how a man who possessed such an amazing gift and who had that much impact on others wasn't more well known.

The group wasn't scheduled to meet Mauricio or Maria Lucia until the next day. Maria Lucia was another healer from Brasil who had accompanied Mauricio, and was going to work with our group during the day. So everyone who had come for this special event had the evening to prepare. Our meeting was relaxed and informal, and there was no pressure. Many of the people spent the night meditating or talking in small groups. Within a few minutes of their arrival that night, my Mom called and asked me to come and meet Mauricio and Maria Lucia. My heart froze. I didn't want to go. I didn't question why I didn't. I just didn't want to go. But why didn't I? Anyone else who had been invited would have gone without hesitation. What was my dilemma? After all, I seemed to be having one. I told Patricia that I wanted to stay, that I was having fun with Linda and it was not possible for me to come now. I was resisting going and had no idea why. My Mom and I went back and forth. She assured me that I could return to my friends as soon as I met her new guests. I argued, but she was insistent and would not accept no for an answer. Eventually I surrendered to her, as I often did. After all the things I had heard about Mauricio, you'd think I would have been anxious to meet him, but I wasn't.

I took my time strolling from the lodge down to the house at the foot of Delphi's little mountain. As I walked into my Mom's house, I saw a strong-featured, rugged but somewhat short man. He was wearing a light blue button down cotton shirt with brown loosely hanging pants. His pure white hair lay messily on his forehead, rather like that of a mischievous little boy, and his smile was infectious, charismatic. You could literally feel it light up the room. But what impressed me most were his eyes. You could sense the magnitude of his soul through them. His eyes could speak without words, and they glowed with a gentle strength. His very presence seemed so familiar to me, and all of the resistance and defensiveness that I had been feeling left me at that moment. When he took my hand to greet me, I felt a sudden and overwhelming sense of humility. Looking stunned, Mauricio gasped and was taken aback. He dropped my hand as if it had burned him and I wondered if I had done something wrong. He looked a bit puzzled, but I dismissed it by making light of the whole thing. We all sat down to talk. We hadn't been sitting down for more than ten minutes when Mauricio suddenly announced that he would work on me. Now it was my turn to gasp. I was not prepared for that. I can't tell you the range of feelings that shot through me in those next few seconds. But I didn't have time to even think of saying no, as he was already leading me into the adjoining room which was set up as a treatment area.

I walked into the room feeling very nervous, but when I lay down on the table and closed my eyes, a feeling of great peace came over me. I remembered my mother's calm. I had the feeling that I was now in the hands of God. How do you describe being in the hands of God? From that moment forward trust was not an issue. I knew that I was safe. Mauricio stood at my head with his index fingers on my temples, speaking phrases in Portuguese. After a few moments, I felt a sweet, gentle love flow through his hands and its fluid warmth filled my body, calming and lifting my mind and emotions. In a low voice he called out, "energía, energía, energía," and I felt my spirit rise up and out of my body. There were no physical bounds to my energy. I felt as though I had no beginning and no end. I could see, create, and experience eternity, all at the same time. Mauricio placed his finger on my third eye, the area of spiritual vision on my forehead, and chanted "la força, la força, la força." A few moments later, huge sparks of blue and white light flashed brilliantly in the room. I could feel the sparks move through me, filling me with their intensity. After a few minutes, he moved to my feet and said, "harmonía, harmonía, harmonía," and again, immense sparks of light filled the room. I could see the lights even with my eyes closed, but had no idea where they were coming from. I didn't really care. Every time a spark emerged, I felt it move through me and as it did, I literally felt my cells, atoms and molecules rejuvenate. With each breath I took, I was more alive and more fully aware of everything in me and around me. I was enfolded in the warm grace of God, and I understood the true limitlessness of Spirit. I felt humbled and honored at the same time.

Again, Mauricio touched my third eye, my sixth chakra, and ripples of energy washed through my body. He called out, "Brother lights, we need your help! Enoch! Uhr! Shallar!" A blue light filled the room and I saw sparks of electricity dancing all around me. The hissing sound that Mauricio used with his kundalini breaths carried me higher and higher in unison with the light. I wondered where it was taking me. I felt my awareness lift even higher. My energy expanded even more, and I became aware of how grand we all are as human beings, and how spiritually connected we are to everything that has existence, even if we are unaware of it. Mauricio's lights were touching places in my soul that had not been awakened for lifetimes. What a sense of belonging, of oneness, and freedom!

After the session was over, it took me some time to get up. I was a little wobbly, and at a loss for words. While Mauricio was recovering his own energy and preparing for the next session, I had time to gather myself and contemplate what had just happened to me. A part of me was blown away. I felt the humility of my experience and it's great magnitude. I didn't really understand what had just occurred, and I didn't really care, at least not enough to analyze it. I walked back into the kitchen and sat down at the table. I was happy just to be. Everything was perfect. I sat there for a long time, enjoying an overwhelming feeling of bliss and watching this demonstration of light and love take place.

Later, when I was finally able to speak, I went back into the room to thank Mauricio. He humbly accepted my thanks and I felt immersed in his love. I felt as though I had touched a God. I experienced a tremendous source of energy that had flowed through us both, he as its channel and me as its receiver. In this feeling of love, I hugged Mauricio and when I did, I felt a strong ache in his heart. I recognized the deep loneliness he was feeling. I had the feeling too that there were things unsettled in his life. I realized that despite his

gift, he was a human being with the same thoughts, fears and insecurities as the rest of us. My compassion went out to him.

Mauricio began working with Patricia, again speaking commanding mantras in Portuguese. Once more the room was alive with energy. Light pulsated everywhere, filling the space with an inexplicable
presence. Even as I watched from outside the room, I was deeply
involved in the energy. My consciousness was totally immersed, experiencing the energization as if I was the one on the table, even though
I wasn't. My perspective had changed but the feeling remained the
same. I was in the presence of God. I could literally feel the divine
presence in the room as Mauricio evoked the lights by calling out his
mantras. And the incredible lights would come to bring healing energy from Spirit through Mauricio to Patricia. I stayed to watch
Mauricio work on Marshall and then on Maria Lucia. Each energization was as powerful as the last. By the time he was finished working
with our little impromptu group, I had lost all sense of time and was
beyond any feelings of responsibility for my friends, who by that time
had given up on me.

Walking back up the mountain to the lodge, I reflected on my
experience. I felt such hope as I looked up to the night sky and its
array of twinkling stars. Everything looked much clearer than when I
had walked down. The beauty of nature, in love and in oneness, surrounded me and I felt my own higher presence walking with me. I
wished that everyone in the world could feel what I was feeling in
that moment. What a world we would all be living in if they did!

We spent the following day learning a spiritualist massage technique from Maria Lucia. During the morning break, I walked out of
the room with Linda to spend a few moments outside. Mauricio was
there waiting. His honeysuckle eyes looked into mine, and I couldn't
help but feel drawn into his presence. I walked over to him. I noticed
that I was gliding over in a very casual way. It felt so natural. We
extended our hands to greet one another. God how familiar he felt.
He said to me, "You are Kimberly." When I answered yes, Mauricio
responded in his broken English, "Your name is like a bell to me. It
sang to me all night long. I had to come now to see if you are real. I
asked Patricia, and she assured me that you were." I smiled, even
though I was puzzled and somewhat surprised. In my work, I was
accustomed to people saying all kinds of things to me, so I didn't give
his statements much thought. I thanked him again for last night and
let him know how happy I was that he would be working with the

group that evening. Then I moved on to do other things. But it wasn't easy. He followed me, and I couldn't get away from him. Nor did I really try. It was true, from that day forward we were like magnets, always being drawn to one another.

Thirty people is a fairly large group, so we set up tables in our new sanctuary side-by-side, so Mauricio could work on four people at once. Even though they were lying next to each other, each person received their own individual energization. During the sessions, many people cried. Everyone felt their energy field expand as they experienced an incredible sense of bliss and peace. Some felt a strong connection to a higher wisdom, and an acceleration of their own personal healing. Not all of them completely understood what had happened, but they all felt this magnificent energy, and a spiritual and cosmic awakening in their bodies. Everyone in the group was awed by their experience. Afterwards, they loved sitting with Mauricio, listening to all of his stories and just being in his energy. That, in itself, was worth the trip.

A friend of mine had come that evening with a brace on his arm, and was scheduled for surgery the very next week. He had been resistant to coming, but I convinced him and inspired him to do so. I also told him to cancel his surgery, because I had the feeling that he wouldn't need to have it after this experience. Although he wouldn't agree to cancel the surgery, he did agree to come. After the energization was over, we had to carry my friend off the table. He was unable to walk, and it took a very long time for his consciousness to come back into his physical body. He was simply stunned, unable to fathom or even explain what he had just experienced, and he was moved beyond tears. I was grateful once again for the beautiful healings that were taking place in our sanctuary. A few hours later, when he was fully aware again and free of pain, he took off the brace on his arm and went home carrying it instead of wearing it. A few days later he cancelled the surgery. To this day he has not had another problem with his arm. Experiences like this are what make this work so rewarding. To "enlighten" means to bring light, whether it is in a thought, a word, or a simple act of kindness. This experience seemed to bring "enlightenment" in every sense.

The next evening, Linda, my friend Bill, Mauricio and I sat down to dinner together at a small table. As we were eating, Mauricio and I gently touched our legs together, as if bumping them, but not on purpose. I had the strangest sensation flow through me. I felt a rush of energy that lifted me very quickly into an altered state. I had no control of my actions. It was like a trance, capturing me totally. I was aware of being in two places at the same time. Linda and Bill were staring at us. They didn't understand what was going on, and for that matter neither did we. Both of us had tears streaming down our faces staring into the air with a far away look. We hadn't looked at each other, so neither one of us knew we were having the same reaction.

Then Linda and Bill and the kitchen itself faded out of my consciousness, as I began to see pictures roll by as if on a movie screen inside my head. This was a new and surprising phenomenon for me, and I was captivated by the scenes I was seeing. I saw a city that was far more futuristic than the cities we know. The buildings appeared as perfect geometric shapes, some with translucent domes. Surely I wasn't crazy, but what I was seeing was as real as day. I recognized the place immediately, but I couldn't remember its name. I saw myself in a laboratory. There were others there too, each focused on his or her particular job. I was a scientist, dressed in a white lab coat engaged in some type of testing work. I sensed that I was fulfilled in my work and appeared to be very dedicated to it. I looked across the room and saw Mauricio, who was also dressed in a lab coat. He saw me and called out my name, "Neika, Neika come here." I was stunned as the recognition washed over me. I realized that I knew him and that I've known him for a very, very long time. I was amazed at what I was seeing and feeling. I felt bound by love, yet freer than I have ever felt. The respect I was feeling for him was ancient. I had always respected Mauricio's scientific nature and I loved learning from him. And I realized in this moment that we had worked together many times before. I felt bigger than life. Incredible surges of love for him flowed through me, and then, like a chord of energy, I was pulled slowly back into my awareness. Tears, so many tears. Tears of joy. Tears of clarity. Tears of release. Knowing but not knowing. Blinded by tears, my body now trembling, I found myself back in the kitchen.

I was in a state of deep love, and for the first time since we sat down to dinner, I looked into Mauricio's deep brown eyes. I was feeling terribly vulnerable and emotional at that point, and I was sure I was a mess, but I didn't care. Looking at him, I could see that he was feeling much the same. He too was shaken up, but his presence emanated such confidence and knowing. His eyes were full of conviction, and now were gazing into mine. It startled me so. I remember fleeing to the shower wanting to brush off this experience quickly. What was I thinking, that I could brush or wash the whole thing off? I had just experienced a deep recognition, and I was greatly moved. But I got scared. This was something beyond my control. I couldn't yet grasp the full meaning of this experience. Was I in denial, or was I just too blind to see what was happening to me. Although I had a strong feeling of devotion and total commitment to Mauricio, the same feeling that I experienced in the laboratory, I also felt a great resistance within me, as I cried uncontrollably. I just didn't understand these feelings.

After dinner, the entire group gathered together in preparation for what was about to come. I was feeling a little concerned for Mauricio and what he was about to do. After all, he was going to light up the top of the mountain at Delphi in order to make contact with his Brother Lights. I knew that he was under pressure. We all walked quietly up the mountain, some of us feeling a bit nervous, others calm and reflective. But there was an excitement in the air. I wasn't certain how I felt about it all at that point. Looking back I realize that I must have been in Mauricio's energy and feeling his nervousness. We all gathered together joining hands and formed a circle at the top of the hill, including Mauricio. We began to chant the mantra "OM." With every breath our love grew stronger, and we were united in oneness. We continued to chant as the energy increased in our group ten fold. You could feel the shifts. After a while, Mauricio quietly left the circle to walk in the woods and make his connection.

I couldn't help but think how unbelievable this all was. Here was this humble man going off into the woods to make contact with his brother lights. It was like we were about to have a UFO experience. I was taking it all very seriously. This was not a show. Mauricio was acting as the intermediary, opening us to other dimensions in the universe through his light. I wanted everyone to concentrate and be serious as me. This was a spectacular moment for all of us, and I know there were some in the group who wondered if these lights would really make contact. I could feel their doubt.

But the energy was conducive and cooperative, and after about ten minutes or so, lights began to dance in the sky. Suddenly, lights were everywhere. As they moved closer to us, we could see them clearly. Some lights were bigger than others. Some were the size of baseballs, and some were smaller. Some shot by us quickly, like shooting stars, and some moved more slowly, with trails, like comets. Some looked like lightning bolts, shooting straight down from the sky into the ground. There were beautiful orange and yellow lights, translucent blue lights, and clear, radiant white lights dancing all around us. Some of the lights came very close to us, as close as five feet, and some stayed far away, moving among and between the trees, up, down and all over the mountain. It looked as if they were interacting with each other, communicating back and forth. Some lights would flash and others would flash in response. It reminded me of the lights in the movie "Close Encounters of the Third Kind." But that was a film and this was real!

We stood in awe and marveled at what we saw as these lights in the sky were dancing all above us and around us. The lights continued for about thirty minutes and then began to leave much as they had come, a few dancing lights at a time. After they had all disappeared, Marshall was looking for Mauricio but couldn't find him. He had not come back to the clearing, and Marshall was concerned over his whereabouts. He started looking for him, calling his name, searching for him everywhere. He finally found Mauricio lying on the dirt road about 50 feet from the woods. He was unconscious, and blood had stained his shirt where some of the lights had burned his chest.

After about five minutes, Marshall was finally able to revive him. Mauricio was groggy and a little bit out of it. They told me that his first words were, "Kimberly, my belle. Where is Kimberly?" He was calling for me. I wasn't close enough to hear him, but my Mom found me saying, "Kimberly, come quickly, Mauricio is calling for you." I didn't understand why he wanted me, but I ran to help. When I arrived, Marshall had already gotten him to his feet. I took one look at him and I wanted to cry. The blood was dripping down his chest from the cross stigmata that had been seered over his heart. The wound was raw, and I knew it had to be painful. My heart went out to him. I didn't understand why he had to endure this. Was seeing the lights that important to us that he had to make this sacrifice? Was it worth it to the people for him to have to endure such an intense experience? I didn't understand why it upset me so. I put his arm around me and supported him as we started down the mountain path.

Quietly we began our descent. About halfway down the mountain, Mauricio stopped. He turned to face me, looked deeply and directly into my eyes, and said, just as calm as day, "Oh, my love, I have been looking for you for 400 years!" I looked at him somewhat shocked, and I took a deep breath to compose myself. By far, that was definitely the best line I'd ever heard! I smiled, trying to make light of it, but I couldn't. Once again I was afraid. It felt like everything was suddenly closing in on me. Part of me wanted to flee, to run back to Delphi, join my friends and pretend this never happened. But when I looked at him, and looked into those deep piercing eyes, I knew he was telling the truth. True to form, I did not show my feelings. With great poise I turned away, and continued helping him down the mountain.

After our return, Patricia wanted me to come to their house again, but I refused. I was feeling even more resistant, especially now that this old man had professed his love for me. But Patricia insisted, and, again I gave in, promising Linda that I would return in short order. Little did I know that this was the night my entire life would change.

As I entered the kitchen of Patricia and Marshall's home, Mauricio looked at me and seemed to understand my discomfort. He made no effort to reiterate his love. His eyes said it all. Instead, he began to joke and I felt a bit more at ease. He certainly had the gift of gab, even with his broken English, and he began to entertain us with great humor, telling stories about his life.

4

Yes I am a dreamer, for a dreamer is one
who can only find his way by moonlight, and
his punishment is that he sees the dawn
before the rest of the world.

—Oscar Wilde

AURICIO'S FATHER WAS a teacher at the Granberry School In Juiz de Fora, Brasil. He was also the Pastor of the Methodist church there, which was affiliated with the school. Joao Baptista Panisset was a serious man, especially when it came to spiritual matters. He believed in all denominations of Christianity, and had the ability to walk into any church and speak their language. He had a strong love and compassion for all people. Sometimes, when he laid his hands on the sick, they became well instantly. Mauricio's father was always ready to help those in need, and this attitude greatly influenced Mauricio in his later life.

Mauricio was an unruly child. Of the six children in the family, he was the only one his parents could not discipline. Mauricio didn't care about school and would play hooky whenever he felt like it. He was adventurous and was always looking for ways in which he could rebel, at times even daring life itself. By the time Mauricio had reached the age of nine, his parents were at their wits end. At age ten he did a simple experiment. He built a homemade bomb that blew away the gate of the Granberry School. Not knowing what to do with their undisciplined son, they sent him to live on his grandparent's farm in a remote place called Colonia. Life on the farm with Manoel and Genuina Guedes was much harder for Mauricio than was his previous carefree life. He had been given many chores that took a long time. And when he was finished, there was always more to do. Mauricio hated chores. Long hours and constant work did not mix well with his fierce independence. His rebellious nature and penchant for doing only as much as he could get away with got him in trouble many times.

In teaching Mauricio discipline, his grandparents imposed certain conditions upon him. He was allowed to ride the fourteen miles to school with his cousin on the horse and wagon. But in the afternoon when school was over, he had to walk back. At first, the long walk back didn't bother Mauricio. The longer he took walking home, the fewer chores he would have to do. So he always took his time on the way home. But one day, Mauricio became so absorbed with killing time, that it got dark before he knew it. By the time he came to the mountainous and wooded part of the walk, it was pitch black. Although Mauricio was somewhat apprehensive about being alone in the woods at night, he was not too concerned about it until he became aware of an unusual glow of light behind him. The glow scared him badly because he knew there were panthers in these woods, and he was sure the light he saw was coming from the eyes of a hungry feline. He began to walk very quickly and then he began to trot, looking back every few minutes to see if the light was still with him. It was. He broke into a run, but each time he looked back the light was still there, always maintaining its interval. He ran about a mile and a half, when he realized that it wasn't a pair of eyes following him at all, but rather, a single ball of blue light! Instead of calming his fears, this frightened him even more, because he couldn't imagine what it could be. He stopped looking back, and concentrated on running as fast as he could. Fear and adrenaline kept him going until, with great relief, he finally reached the safety of the farmhouse.

Mauricio burst into the kitchen where Genuina was just putting dinner on the table and, gasping for breath, tried to tell the family what had happened. The family laughed at his story, not believing a word of it. Manoel failed to see any humor in the story at all. Instead, he gave Mauricio a stern look and berated him for being late for his chores. His grandfather warned that if he missed his chores again, he would be severely punished.

The next morning when Mauricio awoke, he began to think that maybe the family was right. No one else had ever seen anything like that before, and maybe he hadn't seen anything either. He convinced himself that it was all in his imagination, and he shrugged it off. That day at school went smoothly, except for the usual scoldings and slaps he received for inattentiveness and mischief. But when the school day was over, Mauricio's bravado ended with it! As he began the long walk home he hoped with all his heart that "the thing" would not be waiting for him again.

Mauricio covered the first part of his walk quickly, trying to get through the wooded area with as much daylight left as possible. He traveled through the woods swiftly, and soon arrived at the mountainous area, where he had previously seen the light. Only this time Mauricio saw nothing. He was greatly relieved, telling himself, "See, you imagined the whole thing!" As he reached the peak of the mountain and started down, he was feeling confident, and slowed his steps so that he wouldn't get home too early and end up doing extra chores.

But, just as that thought occurred to Mauricio, he sensed something directly behind him. He looked over his shoulder and once again saw the ball of light, the same way it appeared the night before. This time, Mauricio knew it was not his imagination. This was real! He ran, hoping he could outrun it or that it would tire of pursuing him. But just as before, the light maintained its distance and followed him all the way home. True to form, the light disappeared just before he arrived at the farm. Once again he raced into the house, winded and excited, telling the family that the same thing had happened. No one laughed this time. His grandfather was angry and told Mauricio to stop the nonsense. Sensing that he was already very close to a beating, Mauricio decided that regardless of how frightened he was, he had better learn to deal with this "light" on his own, and he didn't mention it again.

The following day was a Saturday, so Mauricio would not have to worry about these strange events for two days. But Monday eventually arrived and the thought of facing the light again was too much for him to bear. So he decided he had two choices: he could run from the light or stop going to school. He chose the latter, and on that Monday morning when he and his cousin were several miles from the farm, Mauricio got off the horse, and extracted a promise from his cousin not to tell his grandfather. Mauricio hid in the fields most of the day and arrived back at the farm at the usual time, but soon found that his plans had backfired. When asked by their teacher where Mauricio was, the cousin told the teacher that Mauricio was playing hooky. The teacher immediately got word to Manoel. Needless to say, Mauricio was back in school the next day, sitting gingerly on a sore backside. But Mauricio was still afraid of the light, so during the last hour of school he faked illness and was allowed to go home on the horse with his cousin. His cousin also had a sore behind due to the beating he received for snitching on Mauricio, and both of them had a rather uncomfortable ride home that day.

Mauricio knew he couldn't feign illness everyday, and decided that his only remaining option to avoid the light was to run from it. The next day after school, he approached the mountains with trepidation, hoping the light wouldn't be there. But the light was there waiting for him, just as it had before. For the next few months, each day was the same. The light was always there to meet him, and it would always follow him, staying just behind him on his right side as he dashed madly through the woods. No matter how many times he ran away from it, it was still there waiting for him the next day. As this continued, Mauricio gradually became accustomed to the light, and even grew to rely on its presence as a sort of companion.

During this time period, Mauricio began to notice changes in his physical body. There were many nights during which he could not sleep due to excess energy. The normally healthy boy started coming down with sudden fevers and other illnesses so severe that doctors were often called in. The doctors rarely found any cause for these surprising illnesses. Mauricio would get well as suddenly as he got sick, much to the chagrin of his uncle who always suspected he was faking.

During one particularly severe episode, Mauricio came down with the flu, which became worse and worse over the course of several weeks, and ultimately developed into a bacterial infection. It became so severe, and his fever so high, that Mauricio was not expected to live. Although gravely ill, Mauricio could still hear and understand the conversations going on around him. He heard his grandfather talking about his imminent death, as the family stood around his bedside. As soon as Mauricio became aware of what they were talking about, he began to get concerned himself about whether he would recover. But at that moment he saw a brilliant blue light come through the wall and hover over his body. Mauricio's grandfather announced to the family that this light was the angel coming to take Mauricio to heaven, and they prepared to say goodbye. Even though the light frightened them, they stood over Mauricio and prayed.

Mauricio knew it wasn't true. The blue light didn't frighten him. This light was just like the one that followed him home from school each day. Then he heard a voice coming out of the light, which spoke to him telepathically of his mission. The light told him that he would get well soon and not to be concerned. The voice then explained to him that his purpose in this life would be to help heal others, and he was being prepared for this life of service. The voice was comforting to Mauricio, and the light hovered over him for several more minutes before it moved away. From that moment on he began to get well. In three days he was out of bed, and within two weeks he was back doing the chores he so much loved to hate.

It was only years later, as an adult, that Mauricio understood the connection of the lights to his illnesses. He told us he was sure that all of these mysterious illnesses were caused by the light energies preparing him and his energy bodies for his healing work. He explained that the lights were working on his kundalini and his chakras, preparing him for the influx of spiritual light that he would direct for the healing of others. He was so humble and earnest as he described his relationship with the lights, and his belief that they kindled within him, at a very early age, the deep desire to create a healing ministry.

One afternoon on the farm, Mauricio was hunting for food with his cousin about a mile from the house. At a nearby creek, they stalked and finally trapped a small animal that was much like a beaver. As they cornered the animal against a large tree, Mauricio hit it over the head with a long stick. Although the animal was knocked unconscious immediately, Mauricio continued to hit it until he was sure it was dead. When he picked the animal up by the hind legs to take it home, he discovered that it was a female, and that she was pregnant. This devastated Mauricio, and his emotions welled up as he began to cry. His cousin ridiculed him for this display, and called him a baby. Mauricio very quietly took the dead animal and put her in his bag to take home with him. His cousin left laughing, leaving Mauricio alone.

Mauricio was beside himself. On the way back to the farm, he tried bargaining with God, promising that he would do anything if only this poor animal and its babies could be saved. When Mauricio arrived back at the farmhouse, he took the dead animal into the corncrib where no one could see him. He gently laid the animal down and placed his hands over its head the same way his father did when he was doing healing work. For a long time, nothing happened, but Mauricio did not give up. He knew that if he were patient enough, believed enough, and if his intention was pure enough, God would help the animal.

After a long time, a small bright blue light suddenly appeared above Mauricio's hands. It hovered there, much the same as the light had hovered over his body when he himself had been ill. Suddenly, the blue light went through his hands and into the body of the animal. After what felt like an eternity, the animal stirred slowly and began to breathe. His miracle had come true. For the rest of the afternoon, Mauricio stayed in the corncrib, putting his hands on the head of the animal, crying, praying, and thanking God. At about six o'clock that evening, the animal stumbled to its feet and ran out of the corncrib and into the woods. Mauricio was ecstatic! But when he finally returned to the house, everyone was angry about his disappearance, and for neglecting his chores. He didn't tell anyone what happened and took his beating without a word.

After a while, there came a time when the light stopped following Mauricio home from school. Instead, it began visiting at other times, and in other situations. One year, the family's sugar cane crop had become infested with insects that caused devastation and death to the plants. This was a grave situation for the family, because sugar cane provided their main income. Every night the family went out into the fields to pray, trying to find hope amid the dying cane. Then, one evening at dusk, as the family walked in the field together, a strange light came out of the sky above them. At first they were shocked into silence, watching as the light hovered over the field. Then some of them became fearful, saying it was a UFO and they were in danger. After a few minutes, the light disappeared into the sky. As suddenly as it left, so did the family's discussion about it. They pretended nothing happened, and they didn't want to talk about it, even to each other, for fear of sounding crazy. But after a few days, the pests were completely gone from the fields and the sugar cane matured to yield a bumper crop.

Still the family refused to discuss the light or the miraculous healing of the cane. They never discussed the connection between the lights and Mauricio, even though the lights chased him home from school, healed his bacterial infection, and cured their sugar cane. In fact, the family never talked about any of the odd events that happened when Mauricio was around. The phenomena scared them, so they just pretended it never happened. Once, Mauricio's grandmother told him to watch over and stir a large pot of stew that was bubbling on the stove. The spoon was made of aluminum, and as Mauricio stood stirring, it became soft and pliable in his hand. Frightened, Mauricio began to hold it very gingerly with only his fingertips, and kept stirring as ordered. But the spoon melted and curled up in his hand. Rather than show his amazement at this phenomenon, his uncle accused Mauricio of deliberately destroying the spoon and severely disciplined him. Experiences like these led Mauricio to develop a dislike of spontaneous phenomena and psychic events. But that didn't stop him from experiencing them.

Many nights while lying in bed, Mauricio heard a voice saying over and over again, "I am Enoch, I am Enoch". He didn't know quite what this voice was or what to do about it. Nor did he associate it with the lights. He just chalked it up as another strange event in his life, one of many. Then one night, Mauricio was inspired to go back to where he had first seen the lights. He didn't know why, but something told him to go. It had been raining that night, but by the time he reached the mountains, the rain had ended. As Mauricio stood in the spot where he first saw the ball of light, a hole opened in the clouds directly above him and three balls of light, about the size of tennis balls, appeared. They were moving diagonally but turned toward him, becoming larger as they got closer, until they were about the size of basketballs. Mauricio was startled and somewhat afraid, but as fast as his heart was beating, he did not have the urge to run like before. As he stood there and watched, the balls came to within thirty feet of him, and he clearly heard a voice say, "I am Enoch, I am Enoch." When he heard the voice, his fears melted away, and his body relaxed. His heart had come alive, for he knew an old friend had come to visit him, the being called Enoch.

When he finished sharing this story with us, Mauricio looked very seriously at me across the kitchen table and said, "Enoch is still with me, coming to me as often as I call him for help. He always comes as a brilliant white light. When Enoch comes, he brings knowledge, healing, or situational changes in one's life." I asked Mauricio if this was the same Enoch as was in the Bible and he assured me that indeed he was.

Mauricio went on to describe his return to his father's house after four years on the farm. According to Mauricio, the homecoming was not very successful because farm life had not taught him the discipline his father had hoped it would. Mauricio still did not care about school other than electricity and physics, the few subjects he did find interesting. Because of his general disinterest in the other subjects Mauricio bounced around, attending three different schools in three years with little success.

During those years the lights continued to manifest, but not near-ly as often. The lights seemed to come to him just enough to let him know that they were close. Mostly the light would come when he was doing a healing on someone who had a good measure of spiritual evolvement, or who was a person of good character.

When Mauricio had returned home from the farm, he was driven to make a small healing room down in the basement of his father's house. He was intrigued with the thought of healing. It came so nat-ural to him. As young as he was, the experience on the farm deep-ened his love and desire to help others. It didn't matter who or what he was healing. He was very conscientious and responded wherever there was a need. Many times he took his own food from the dinner table to feed some of his hungry patients down in his healing room.

Mauricio never told his family about what he was doing. He did-n't want to get into trouble, especially after the ridicule and beatings he took on the farm. And he was silent about the unusual phenom-ena that were taking place in his life. He had no one to share with, and oftentimes he felt isolated from others. Through his experiences he became more and more comfortable with his own abilities to heal. Finally, he wanted to tell someone. He was ready to share, and he felt that if anyone would understand, it would be his father, who he trusted. So with some hesitancy, he broached the subject in con-versation. Mauricio told his father everything that had happened on the farm, and about the healing work that he was now doing in his father's basement.

To Mauricio's astonishment, his Father was calm and composed. After looking deeply into his son's eyes, he said to him, "I am not surprised by what you tell me. I always knew you would have a spe-cial gift some day." His father had known all along what he was doing in that basement. He even knew that Mauricio often gave his food to others. The reaction of his father was much more of a surprise to Mauricio than the other way around. Mauricio looked at him for a long time, silent and dumbfounded. He had expected rejection but instead his father began to counsel him on the use of his spiritual gifts. He cautioned Mauricio that such gifts were from God and should be used only for spiritual and healing purposes. He told him stories of how Jesus healed, reminding him that Jesus said we are all healers and could do everything he did. His father was pleased, and from that day onward Mauricio saw a marked change in his attitude towards him, even though he was still a very independent teenager.

With his father's support and encouragement, Mauricio was inspired to continue his healing work. He had a great love for healing, and a tremendous desire to help others.

As time passed and Mauricio grew older, he came to realize that he needed an education if he ever wanted to get a good job. So now he focused his attention on his mental and intellectual development. Since he had failed most of his previous schoolwork, he had a lot of catching up to do. Rather than laboriously plodding through the regular school curriculum, he enrolled in an accelerated school in Rio de Janeiro where, if he kept his grades up, he would be granted credit for three years of schooling in just one year. During his time at the accelerated school, Mauricio was not interested in spiritual things and the lights moved into the background, allowing him the opportunity to finish his education. Occasionally, they would flash just to let him know they were still around.

Mauricio applied himself vigorously and completed two sessions in just under two years. After he finished his schooling, Mauricio went into the army for two years, as was legally required in Brasil. Then he took the Vestibular, a local examination that tests students' skills in many areas. Mauricio got the highest score on the test for engineering, and chose that as his course of study. After a year or two, although he hadn't finished his engineering courses, he applied to work at the government's telecommunications corporation. Since he was already considered a genius in the field, the Minister hired him on the spot. Mauricio accomplished a great deal here. It was largely because of his talent and hard work that the World Cup was broadcast in color throughout Brasil for the first time.

Eventually, Mauricio went to work for the Banco do Brasil in Juiz de Fora during the day, while satisfying his urge to tinker with electricity and electrical things at night. At that time, television reception was not possible in Juiz de Fora, because the mountains surrounding the town blocked the signals from the TV networks in Rio de Janiero. Many engineers had tried to create a device that could receive the signals through the mountains, but none had succeeded until Mauricio put his abilities to work. Mauricio's father always paid for his taxi trips so that he could go to the Morro do Imperador, where he did all the final testing of his equipment. After his invention had proven successful, the mayor gave a party at which they would throw the main switch that would turn on TV in Juiz de Fora. Although this was all a surprise to Mauricio, he attended the party anyway, and threw the main switch himself. It was such an accomplishment that a picture of the mayor with Mauricio was published in the Rio de Janeiro newspaper. Mauricio, who was such a private person, would never have agreed to such self-promotion if he had known what was coming.

Mauricio later left Juiz de Fora, but stayed with the Banco do Brasil, working first in Rio de Janeiro and later in Brasília. He moved to Brasília in 1960, when the district capital was being dedicated by then President Juscelino Kubitchek. The sixties were a time of turmoil in Brasil, and in March 1964, leftist President João Goulart was overthrown by the Brasilian armed forces, and sent into exile in Uruguay. The coup, though supported by the upper classes and industrialists, was called a revolution and the military swore it would stay in power until national reconstruction was achieved.

The region was very sensitive about actions that might be viewed as Communistic, and the Brasilian military took the same view. These were the Kennedy/Johnson years, and the U.S., through the Alliance for Progress, was funneling money into Central and South America hoping to avert further Communist takeovers such as the one that happened in Cuba. In Brasília, Mauricio was openly urging the Candangos, Brasilians who had relocated to help build the new capital, to demand better living and working conditions. But his actions were viewed as subversive by the military, and Mauricio was arrested and jailed, charged with being a Communist.

Mauricio's brother Ulysses was a Major in the Brasilian Army. He was a loved and trusted father figure as well as a big brother to Mauricio. He knew he had to get Mauricio out of jail as soon as possible because if he didn't intervene, Mauricio would have been there a lot longer, or he might have simply "disappeared." When he heard his brother had been jailed, Ulysses immediately left a birthday party in Minas Gerais and headed for Brasília. Ulysses had a good relationship with the members of the government at the time and was able to free Mauricio, but not before his brother had been beaten and tortured.

It was in jail that Mauricio first questioned God. He was angry at God, angry at his circumstances, angry with the treatment and interrogation he received, and angry at the injustice and suffering of the people of Brasil. He wondered what kind of God would allow such things to happen and place him in these circumstances. But it was in jail where his resistance would be broken down, and the groundwork laid for his spiritual mission. Every servant of God must pass through a catharsis in order to prepare them for what is to come. It is only through these difficult tests and challenges that God can mold us into the person that we would otherwise never be. After his release, no one would associate with Mauricio, even though he was in jail for only a short time. People were afraid that if they did, then they too would be made out to be Communists, and be arrested themselves. Mauricio lost what friends he had. He lost his apartment. He lost his credit. He lost everything, and had to start his life over, feeling even more isolated and alone.

Mauricio went back to work. He worked on many of the projects being built in Brasília including the radio tower, a massive structure of concrete and steel. One afternoon Mauricio got careless and fell twelve stories to the ground. He thought he was going to die or at least be seriously injured. But as he fell, a cloud of soft light enveloped him, holding him, helping to smooth his fall. Telepathically a voice spoke to him and reminded him of his mission, and the healing work that he should be doing. When he finally landed, he had fractured a leg, but that was the worst of it. He had fallen twelve stories and had only a broken leg to show for it! Mauricio was truly humbled. He knew the fall was a sign, and that he needed to return to his healing ministry. His life was simply out of balance. It seemed that whenever he became occupied with purely mental pursuits or consumed by his job, something would occur that would remind him of his path, the path of healing. He might become ill or suffer an accident that would jolt him out of complacency, and bring him back to the realization that he needed to focus on fulfilling his mission. Mauricio recognized the fall from the tower as one of these events.

The cloud of light that enveloped him during his fall not only reminded him of his mission, but also gave him the ability to access the Akashic Records, the records of each person's past, present and future lives, and the spiritual lessons and growth experiences obtained from those lives.

After Mauricio's experience, the lights drew closer to him and phenomena began occurring on a daily basis. He realized he would have to become much more serious about using his gifts to help others. Soon after, the lights came to him with such power that Mauricio could no longer ignore their message. The light he knew as Enoch told him that he must use his own light to heal the sick in the hospitals of Brasília, and that he should start immediately.

Mauricio resisted. He sometimes doubted his own ability. And he was afraid. He was afraid that the light wouldn't come at his command. He was afraid that there would be people who he wouldn't be able to heal. He worried that he would only raise the hopes and expectations of people who could not be healed because it wasn't in their highest interest. But he was most afraid of what people would do to him because of his gifts. Would they lock him away in an asylum? Would they consider his work to be of the devil and persecute him because of it? These were his fears. And there was an inner conflict as well. Mauricio knew deep down that by accepting and embracing his gift, he would become responsible to use this gift to help others, and in doing so, his life would no longer be his own.

His health did not improve until he finally gave in and went to the hospital to begin his healing work. He made sure that his first visit was very casual, walking down the hall and pretending that he was just there to visit someone. But when he saw so many sick people his compassion prevailed. He wanted to help them and knew that he could. Mauricio paused at the door of each room to feel the energy and sense whether he should enter the room or not. After a few false starts, he felt compelled to enter one of the rooms. As he did, the woman in one bed smiled at him. He walked over to her side and picked up her hand. As he held the woman's hand, he could see her life and her illness in her blood. She closed her eyes, and Mauricio held his hand over her head. Then he gently put his finger on her third eye, and when he did, lights flashed. She lay there with her eyes closed and a smile on her face as he left the room. The others in the room, who hadn't paid any attention until the lights flashed, just watched him go. Their eyes were open very wide, but no one said a word.

As Mauricio continued down the hall he felt inspired. He was assured that he was in the right place, doing what he was supposed to do. Eager to heal, he went back to the hospital the next night and every night thereafter, sometimes working until three or four in the morning. In time, he got to know many of the nurses and doctors, and became familiar with many of the patients. One night he came upon a fourteen year-old girl suffering with brain cancer that wasn't expected to make it through the week. Mauricio entered the room where she lay with her eyes closed. She had already lost all of the hair on her head as well as her eyebrows from the chemotherapy. Mauricio's compassion was strong, and he was compelled to help this girl. He knew without a shadow of a doubt that the light would heal this girl. He worked on her for a long time that night, and returned every night for the next two weeks. After fourteen "energizations" the girl was still alive.

But the next week Mauricio could not go to the hospital. When he finally made it back, he went immediately to her room. He stood in the doorway, shocked and heartbroken to see her bed empty. He had been so sure that this light would heal her and the sight of that empty bed filled him with doubt and despair. He was distraught, because he knew without a shadow of doubt that this girl would and could be healed. He hurried down the hall to the nurses' station to question them. The nurse on duty told him that the girl had been feeling so much better that her mother had checked her out of the hospital and had taken her home.

Mauricio was shocked and at the same time ashamed of the doubt that he felt. He had known all along that the healings would save her life. Why did he experience so much doubt when he saw the empty bed? Mauricio obtained the girl's address. A month or so later when he arrived at her house, the girl who opened the door was unrecognizable to him. Gone was the deathly pallor he remembered, and in its place were rosy cheeks, a happy smile, and most surprisingly, an entire head of beautiful hair! Even her eyebrows had grown back. She recognized him and kissed him, her bright eyes shining with the knowledge that he had saved her life. Mauricio was elated, he was moved, and it humbled him once again to realize that he had allowed his personal doubt to cloud his faith. It was a big lesson for him, one he never forgot. And that lesson helped him to become more detached about his personal feelings. He became less invested in the outcome and relied more upon his intuition. As healers, we can only bring God's light and love to others. It is up to the person to receive it.

In the hospitals Mauricio became known as a healer, but he purposely avoided any notoriety or being singled out for his phenomena. He turned down invitations to appear on TV to demonstrate his lights, because the probability of being labeled a witch or a fake was much stronger than the possibility of being taken seriously, either scientifically or by the general population. Once, his brother Ulysses invited Mauricio to demonstrate his phenomena to a group of scientists and psychiatrists. Although they were astonished by his powers, nothing ever came of their discussions to investigate further. Mauricio had already known that nothing would come of it. Healers who exhibit phenomena and other paranormal events are very common in parts of Brasil, but have never been taken seriously enough to be explored by scientific means. In his hometown of Juiz de Fora, Mauricio was known more for his electronics skills than for his unusual powers.

In 1985 in Brasilia the electronically operated cathedral bells were inoperable, and unable to toll the death of its president. Mauricio climbed the bell tower and activated the bells, somehow making them ring. He had problems moving his hands for about two weeks after that. The incident was so unusual that it was reported in a popular national magazine.

After beginning his healing ministry, Mauricio became a teacher next, and taught at the schools of Elefante Branco and Dom Bosco in Brasília. Eventually he took a job with the government, a civil service position with the ministry of Justice in Brasilia. He worked during the day and concentrated on his healing work at night. He worked to understand these lights and what role they played in healing.

For the next nine years, Mauricio explored and came to understand the invisible worlds and how energy can be utilized for the purpose of healing. He diligently studied the Kaballah, spiritualism, and esoteric teachings, and his long association with the Freemasons helped him in his research and experimentation. He took his studies very seriously, and under the tutelage of an old and very learned gentleman, his knowledge of spiritual matters grew considerably. This knowledge expanded him. He began to understand how materialization and dematerialization took place, gaining greater insight into how he could use his unusual powers to bring light and spiritual awareness into the world. Mauricio progressed through the levels of study, and after many years, became a Mason in the thirty-third degree, the highest honor bestowed by the Freemasons.

We landed with a jolt, and everyone began applauding. It was a Brasilian custom to applaud after landing, a custom that I had grown to love. Whether it was a good landing, or a not so good one, the Brasilians always applauded, just for the mere fact that they arrived safely. I would always love that custom. It is what I loved most about Brasilians, their passion for life. They were not afraid to express themselves and their feelings. Their love of life is something we could learn much about in the United States.

No matter how you slice it, this trip was a grueling one. It took at least twenty-four hours from the time you left to when you arrived at your final destination. But I did have one thing to look forward to on this leg of the journey and that was the duty-free shopping. It would be fun to look around in all the shops. I missed that kind of action, and I was determined to enjoy it. We still had a ways to go and I still had time to gather myself for this re-entry into my new life back in the United States.

Boarding the second plane was almost as difficult as the first. The second one felt even more final, because now we were actually leaving the country. There was no turning back. I could feel the anticipation of not knowing what was to come. In many ways I felt like a child, open and innocent, but not really knowing what I was doing. Then on the other hand I felt like I had lived a hundred years. But I could feel a force of energy guiding me, leading me home. It was a strange feeling, as if home in the U.S. is where I always should have been. And now some invisible force was leading me back where I belonged. We settled in and I lay back to rekindle the memories that were so close to me now.

5

*It is not by the gray of the hair that one knows
the age of the heart.*

–Edward Bulwer Lytton

BACK IN MY mother's kitchen, Mauricio's stories continued. As the night wore on, my defenses had completely fallen away. I was so enraptured in our conversation that I lost all sense of time. I wasn't even aware that Patricia and Marshall had gone to bed. It was like being in another dimension. I understood Mauricio's broken English, and I could relate perfectly with him. We were communicating telepathically. We understood what was being said before the actual words came out. It was just too strange to be dealing with all at once. He was fifty-eight years old and I was only thirty-two. This couldn't be right. I wasn't ready to be with any man, I thought, let alone an older one. Yet, the magnetic pull I was feeling was beyond any control I might have had. It was true—there was nothing to control. There was no need. I felt at home. I felt free to express myself fully. I found it easy to open up just as he did. The intimacy we shared in that night opened my soul. Unbeknownst to me, I was falling in love.

About four o'clock that morning, with thoughts of my friends long gone, I laid down on the sofa in Patricia and Marshall's den. I was exhausted and I had a headache. The last thing I remember was Mauricio drawing circles on my forehead to ease the pain. It was soothing and put me into a deep sleep. The next thing I knew, it was seven a.m. and I awoke with Mauricio sitting on his knees on the floor in front of the sofa, watching me sleep. His eyes were piercing with tenderness, full of so much love. In his deep Brasilian voice he quietly said, "Bom Jeer!" which I understood as "good morning" in

Portuguese. I was so comfortable that it made me uneasy. It didn't seem fair that someone could get that close to me and in such a short time. I soon realized that I hadn't returned to my friends, and I wondered what they would be thinking. Even more embarrassing, Patricia and Marshall were sleeping upstairs. What would they think? Mauricio must have read my mind. He was concerned that I was upset he was there. He assured me that everything was okay, and that he did not sleep. He had been on his knees for the past three hours sending healing energy to me as I slept. The last thing that he wanted to do was to offend Patricia, Marshall, or me, and he was making sure that I understood that. How could I have been upset or put off by finding him there? I was baffled by his innocence. He was child-like in so many ways, yet he gave you the kind of respect that could only come from a wise and mature man. He looked at me as if he knew everything there was to know about me, and more. His compassion was overwhelming. I looked into his eyes, and was filled with the deepest feeling of love I had ever known. He was an angel. His heart was so pure.

Mauricio changed his plans and stayed at Delphi. We were together from that moment forward. We wanted to be together forever. We didn't know how we were going to do it, but we knew we couldn't be apart. There were so many obstacles in our way, and the odds were stacked against us. He lived across the world, in a place completely different from my home in the United States. Mauricio had a life in Brasil, a job, family, not to mention his healing work in the hospitals, or the Foundation he dreamed of building. And I had my own commitments too. I had children, family, my own healing practice, and had started to put down roots in McCaysville. I needed this man in my life like I needed another hole in my head!

But the most serious obstacle facing me was that I was in love with a fifty-eight year old man. Who was going to accept that? I was nervous about what others would think. There were only a handful of people that didn't think I was crazy for loving this old man, but many others thought I had gone off the deep end. They judged me by society's standards, and not by the love in my heart. They just couldn't believe or trust that I had found my true love and that the age difference simply did not matter. So what if we were born at different times? We had found each other! There was nothing to do but take it one step at a time, overcome the obstacles, and let our destiny unfold. We had no choice but to join hands, hold our heads high, and walk forward as if we knew exactly what we were doing. Our time together was precious and we were going to make the most of every moment.

Eventually, Mauricio would have to go back to Brasil where he was the Director of the Federal Police in the Tribunal Government Building in Brasília. He was allowed time off, but could not stay away forever. As it was, he had canceled his flight back several times and ended up staying for a month. But all too soon the day of his departure was at hand. I'll never forget the drive to the airport and the deep sadness we both were feeling. I felt as if part of me was being ripped out of my heart. When we arrived at the gate, Mauricio and I couldn't stop hugging, and we were both crying uncontrollably. He couldn't let go. I couldn't let go. And in that moment I knew what it meant to love someone deeply, with all your heart and soul. A part of me was leaving with him, and I was overwhelmed at the loss.

Mauricio was the last to board the plane and, when they finally shut the door, I stood there with my Papa and wept, and wept, and wept. I was so grateful to have Marshall there with me. He understood and knew what I was feeling. He had such compassion. He embraced me and his hug supported me until I could stand on my own. I still didn't understand what was happening to me. I had never had that kind of reaction over anyone before, where I could not control my feelings. I later found out that Mauricio had the same reaction, and had cried all the way back to Brasil. The two-hour drive back home felt like an eternity. I had three weeks to go before I would see my love again. I didn't think I could wait.

Three weeks later, Patricia, Marshall, and Emmy and Lenny Chetkin accompanied me to Brasil. Mauricio was there to meet us when we got off the plane in Brasília. At last, we were together again. It was hard to contain my excitement. Mauricio insisted on taking us to his foundation site, so the six of us packed into his tiny car for the two-hour drive to the land outside of Brasilia. This was a primitive place. We drove through the sparsely populated jungle area where there were very few homes or people. Finally we arrived at his land, to the place where Mauricio wanted to build his center. At that time, the site was only raw earth with a rocky acropolis of seven giant rocks at the top of the hill, and a small house at the bottom. But the place had a magical and mystical feel to it, and you could sense a vast and primal power radiating from the ground.

This was my first trip to Brasil, and I could have stayed here forever. I could feel surges of energy throughout my body as I followed

Mauricio to the top, the place he called his "contact spot." He explained that his contact spot is where he meets and communicates with his cosmic friends. I couldn't get over how incredible the energy here felt. Mauricio told us that his Brother Lights would communicate by sending lights to us, but we might have to sit and wait for them half the night. We were all quite willing and very excited. No wonder Mauricio loved this place so much. He looked like a young boy, sending lights out from his body to let his cosmic friends know we were there and waiting for them.

Mauricio's energy was always fortified by this land, and his energy and light increased tenfold when he was there. Once we got to the top, we all chose a different rock to sit upon while we waited. Mauricio was walking around the site doing his thing, and I was sitting by myself on one of the rocks meditating. I was feeling absolutely calm and free, totally immersed in nature, when I was compelled to open my eyes. I looked up and saw the Pleiades, the star constellation known as the Seven Sisters, named for the seven stars that form it. I could not take my eyes off these stars. As I watched, the stars became immense, and then I heard the most beautiful celestial music, unlike any I heard before. I'd heard music like this before, but this was different. This was a cosmic symphony, the Harmony of the Spheres, playing just for me. Then, right before my eyes, I saw three lights shoot out from the stars, first yellow, then blue, then green. The music got stronger and my only thought was that I was being called to go home. I must have been in a trance-like state, because without even thinking about it, I got up and began to walk, towards the music, towards my cosmic home.

I never thought about how far away or how far up in the night sky the music was. I just knew I wanted to go there. I must have walked a mile into the jungle when Mauricio found me. He had come after me and was very frightened and upset that I took off walking alone at night. There were panthers here, and snakes, and God knows what else. He told me never to do that again. But I wasn't afraid. I wasn't worried about living in the jungle, and I wasn't worried about the dangers either. I knew I was safe. In fact, I had never felt so secure in all my life. The experience made me realize that I had found my new home here, and my place with Mauricio.

When Mauricio and I returned, Patricia and Marshall were sitting on the rocks and little orange lights were moving all around them in the bushes below. I was excited, asking, "What are those?" Mauricio replied casually, "Oh, those are only elementals." Elementals are thought forms, or bodies of thought that form around our most intense feelings. They often become the foundation of our primary identity, our sense of who we are. I said, "Well okay, Mauricio, but why are they here?" I knew what elementals were, but wondered why we could see them. He said "elementals are thought-forms of ourselves which take on luminescent form. They appear as light entities because they move and jump across the ground. But they never talk to you because they are just thought-forms." He also said that elementals manifest themselves in that way in Brasil because of the preponderance of intense emotions and raw, spleen-like energies in the country. He explained that we were actually seeing our own thoughts or elementals formed through our prayers and expectations. He also acted like it wasn't any big deal. But for me to actually see these elementals moving all around on the ground because of our thoughts was most impressive. If nothing else, these elementals confirmed the reality of the power of thought. We finally went back to our hotel in the wee hours of the morning. We spent all of our evenings at the foundation, and by the end of the trip, I had seen the inexplicable and I had experienced the mystical. How could I ever explain what happened to me? I thought about that. Many would believe me because they know me and trust me. They would feel the truth through my words and experience. How many others would just smile and dismiss my tales as being too farfetched to be true?

On the last evening of our visit, we each stood upon a rock and chanted. We sang while Mauricio sent his light to make contact. We were having a good time while waiting for something to happen. Suddenly, what appeared to be a lightning bolt came down from the sky and dissipated around us. Then other lights came too. Emmy stretched out her arms and a ball of white light came right into her hand. She wasn't frightened. She acted as if this kind of phenomenon happened every day of her life. She had the most beautiful smile on her face as she stood holding this magnificent ball of light. She held it for only a few seconds, and then it sparked away from her. She jumped up and down with joy, like a kid with a new toy. I had not seen her that happy the whole trip. What an adventure we were having! The energy brought by the lights was buoyant, as if the lights were happy to be there with us. They inspired in us a feeling of deep love and an infinitely close connection to Spirit and the universe. We stood in awe of the lights and the power of God. It was an awesome experience.

Finally, it was time to return to the States. I missed my children, but I was also heartbroken at the thought of leaving Mauricio again. The first time he left me was traumatic enough. Mauricio was sad and distraught too. The morning of our departure, while he and I were talking, he announced on the spur of the moment that he was coming with me. He couldn't bear for us to be apart again. I couldn't believe it. Now, I was certain that this man was either crazy or madly in love with me. It was hard to distinguish which. He had a job in Brasil, and an important one at that. How long could he neglect it? Wouldn't they be upset? But he was already on the phone with the airlines and sure enough, we all went home together.

Back in McCaysville, Mauricio and I moved into a little cabin in the woods that I called our cabana. The cabin was located on our white water river, and we were completely enveloped by our surroundings. The energy of the river invigorated Mauricio, especially with all the natural elements of the forest. And the place was remote enough that Mauricio felt safe and secure. His "lights" were at home, too. I was unbelievably happy and contented, and my children quickly warmed up to Mauricio. He was patient and had a wonderful tolerance for little children, especially mine. My boys Patrick and Marshall loved his childlike qualities and his consistency with them. And they loved the phenomena that happened whenever he was near, like the forks and spoons that curled up or melted in his presence, and the objects that came out of the walls or flew across the room. Mauricio could wave his hand with a spiraling sweep, and out of thin air there would appear in his hand a metal object to present to the children. The objects were usually round, like medals, with an outline or picture of Jesus or the Mother Mary on them. The children were always curious and wanted to know more. They wanted Mauricio to teach them all about this magic so that they could do it too. They thought he was quite brilliant.

I never questioned the phenomena. I only knew that it happened because of Mauricio and I accepted it as part of his reality. The lights never hurt anyone, so why should I worry? After awhile, I saw so much phenomena that I didn't always pay attention to it. It didn't seem to matter. The lights and the energy he brought had only one purpose, and that was to help others. Whether it was to bring knowledge, healing, or situational changes, the light always brought an expansion of consciousness and growth.

It appeared that the lights had a special relationship with the boys too. One night, Marshall and Patrick were home with the baby sitter.

Patrick had not been feeling well, and by the time we arrived home he was burning up with fever. At that time the boys shared a room and each of their beds had a window over it. Mauricio asked me to take the babysitter home so he could sit with Patrick and help him. He sat on the bed and soon a soft current of energy began to flow through his hands into Patrick. But Mauricio was uncomfortable, sensing something different. Then he saw what he thought were the lights of my car in the distance coming down the dirt road and thought, "Kimberly drove too fast. She is back too soon." As the lights got closer they appeared to come directly through the woods rather than following the road.

When I returned home and found Mauricio, he was trembling. He told me what had happened. When the lights got closer they merged into one big ball of blue light. Then the ball of light came very quickly through the window into Mauricio, and then instantaneously into Patrick, filling him with a beautiful blue light. At that moment, both boys awoke smiling, saying, "Papa, the light is here," and immediately went back to sleep. Mauricio was more than curious. He was shaken up. He had had no intention of bringing lights for Patrick's healing. So he knew the lights weren't his own. Mauricio was always very careful with children because he was never sure what effect his lights would have on them. Children's chakras are not fully developed until they are about twelve years old, so he never healed them with light. Instead he healed them with energy he channeled, and his energy was always sufficient. "Whose lights are they?" he wondered. "Where did they come from? How is it possible?" Although he was up most of the night contemplating this experience, Mauricio never got an answer. But by the next morning, Patrick's fever was gone, and you never would have known that he was sick at all.

Mauricio knew that the lights came easily for the boys and thought the children were connected to them in some way. He loved the openness the boys had for the lights. One afternoon while I was taking a shower and Mauricio was outside chopping wood, the lights came from outside the window into the living room where Marshall and Patrick were playing. As the lights danced all around them, the children got very excited and came running into the bathroom. They were going a mile a minute, telling me to come out quickly because God was here, and they wanted me to meet him too. "Come see him now, mommy." I laughed. Their shining eyes were so full of innocence, and in a sense I knew they were speaking the truth.

6

Heaven can be inherited by every man who has
heaven in his soul.

–Confucius

IT WASN'T LONG before Mauricio and I created a new life
together. After a few months in the U.S., Mauricio decided he
wanted to retire a year early from his government job in Brasil.
He wanted to build a home in the United States, and put down roots
in Georgia. And he wanted me to work with him, assisting him in
arranging travel and logistics, and by preparing the people for his
healings. During that time, I had been traveling a great deal, and I
was also my mother's right hand at Delphi, teaching classes and
directing student relations. But I gradually reduced my responsibilities there so that Mauricio and I could work together. We knew we
had the ability to create the work we wanted, and we decided that we
could have the best of both worlds. We would live and work together in both the United States and Brasil, developing a healing ministry
in the U.S. that would help support Mauricio's dream, the Fundação
Enoch (Enoch Foundation) in Brasil.

The Enoch Foundation would be a center where Mauricio's scientific interests could progress, a place of study, investigation and exploration into the paranormal. But more importantly, it also included a
school where forty children could live and study. In Brasil, many of
the children are uneducated or undereducated. And since they are
not taught a trade or how to work with their hands, they often grow
up with the faulty idea that it is easier to ask for money than to work
for it. It was nothing to see a four-year-old in the middle of a busy
intersection, holding an infant and begging for money while their

57

mother hid across the street behind the bushes. This situation made Mauricio angry and often left him feeling helpless. He wanted the Foundation to be a place where children could learn a different way of living. Their studies at the Foundation would include academics, and they would also learn how to make the best use of the land. He wanted them to learn practical skills so they would be able to get good jobs. Over time, the children's innate abilities and spiritual gifts would also be developed. They would be taught to be of service to the world while becoming strong leaders who could help lift the consciousness of Brasil and create a more productive country.

For me the dream of a special school for children was an easy one to accept and work at, because I already loved working with young people, and had spent much of my life doing so. I began visiting all the children in the different orphanages in and around Brasilia. The children were wonderful. They thought that Patrick, Marshall, and I were angels from the sky. They were always very eager to see us. One of my favorite orphanages was in Luziania, and we went there all the time. One day while we were visiting, a three-year old boy was in pain and crying for help. My heart went out to him and I asked the director what was the matter with him. She told me that he had a birth defect. His brain was growing too fast and he would only live for another year, two at the most. Without even thinking, I asked if I could do a healing on him. She agreed and went to get the others because she wanted everyone to watch. At the time I wasn't sure why she had to gather them, but I didn't care. It wasn't a show. I just wanted to be with the boy and help him.

A few minutes into the healing the people formed a circle around the young boy and me. Mauricio was standing directly behind me and I knew he was sending his energy, too. The energy in the room increased and the air began to crackle, like static electricity being sparked. Suddenly from the ceiling above us small lightening bolts flashed into the room, and came down through my hands and into the child. It was a riveting moment. Everyone was stunned, including me. Mauricio later said that the mouths of some of the women literally dropped open when it happened. The boy had been so fidgety in his body, and he was in a great deal of pain. But when the light went into him, he calmed down immediately. He smiled an angelic smile. His eyes were different and I knew somehow when I looked at him that he understood what was happening. This child had the eyes of an old man, and at that moment, he seemed to know as I did, that his suffering was a karmic choice he carried into this life. After the healing he was no longer in pain and had a peace about him. I was deeply moved by this experience. I felt humbled, knowing I had so much more to learn.

I learned a lot living in Brasil. My second stay and the children's first stay there lasted four months. On the Foundation land we lived a simple life. There was no room there for my spoiled self. The land was virgin except for a tiny little house that we shared with the bats. We slept on the floor on mattress beds, and at night I had to clear out the bats, or the children wouldn't go to sleep. Our neighbors were big black snakes and other creatures of the jungle, and the panthers always came around in the night. I was never afraid of panthers. Several times we would come upon one of them, and we just stood there staring at each other, eye-to-eye. Nobody dared to move. Then Mauricio or one of the kids would break the spell and the panther would just leave. They never bothered us.

There were no modern conveniences in this place and I soon learned to adapt to cold showers and no electricity. The house had water only because of a water wheel built laboriously by Mauricio, which carried water up the mountain from the river. Our toilet was also connected to the wheel. I can't remember how many times we had to go to the bathroom outside and then bury it because the water wheel stopped working. I can remember laughing, wondering what I had gotten myself into.

But I didn't care. I was happy and I was content. I could have lived anywhere, and four months isn't a lifetime. So for all of us it became an adventure. The cold showers were even bearable, especially in the afternoon, because it was so hot and dry. I loved waking up in the wee hours of the morning just to hear the parrots chirping away. Each morning I could walk just outside my door and pick leaves off the trees for our morning tea. I got to know these trees well. I picked leaves from a different tree each day, so I was able to learn about the healing effects of each of them. The tea was very soothing, and always calmed my nerves. I loved the simplicity of life here, in harmony with nature, the way life should really be lived. At the foundation, I was enveloped by the natural, beautiful, and raw elements of the earth, and I felt a deep kinship with nature and with the Divine.

It felt so close to heaven here. It was as if you could just reach out and touch the stars. They were so close and so bright, and I loved sitting with Mauricio every night and communing with the celestial bodies. We loved sharing our ideas and our potential for the future. It all felt so clear and possible. During those nights, looking up at the stars, Mauricio shared himself with me. He shared his knowledge and wisdom, his love and his sadness, and even his hope and desire for the world. His experience was so rich, much deeper than mine, even with all the many experiences I'd had in my own life. There was no comparison. I marveled at the knowledge and deep insight Mauricio possessed about the mysteries of life, and I enjoyed learning all that he had to teach me.

He often spoke of the myriad of different galaxies in our universe, worlds within worlds, only occupying other dimensions than our own. He spoke about extraterrestrials and UTs, ultra dimensional beings, and the difference between them. He said that many Brasilians referred to UFOs as Ovinis. In Brasil it was not uncommon to see a UFO of some kind. Maybe it was a silly question but I asked him if they were real or not. Ovinis contacts are real, and more than that, they hold the key to the beginning and ending of civilization, as we know it. To question Mauricio about the reality of such beings would always evoke a smile from him. To him it was ludicrous to question something that was so real and such an intimate part of his daily life.

There are books published today that give facts, accounts, and descriptions of ET visitations from ages past. When the religious vernacular is stripped away, they become very real accounts of ET events. For instance, many believe that the Star of Bethlehem was really a lightship sent to guide seekers to the newly born Christ. How many thousands of people have reported seeing UFOs? And yet, so many doubt their existence, and the existence of anything that lies beyond our world. If you could strip away the veils from your spiritual vision, the veils that allow for our earthly perception of reality, you would be astounded at what you would see in the sky and upon the earth. Mauricio said that ETs are those beings that come to the earth via mechanical means, but with the knowledge and ability to dematerialize and materialize at will, and travel at speeds that far exceed the speed of light. UTs or Ultra Terrestrial Beings are higher spiritual beings who work unseen in our midst for the forces of good. They do not require mechanical means or conveyances to appear on earth. They come and go as they desire by the pure force of will. Because the earth is in a lower state of awareness and perception, the ET gets the greater attention. But most of the influences that come upon earth are Ultra Terrestrial. The UTs operate behind the scenes doing the work of spirit. They work parallel to our world. The UTs are the ones that worked primarily with Mauricio.

During this time I became familiar with Mauricio's "Brother Lights." Each of these lights had its' own vibration and purpose. Mauricio explained that each light was a different entity, and he could never tell which, if any, lights would come when he did his light energizations. Enoch, of Biblical fame and whose name in Hebrew means, "One who initiates into light," was Mauricio's most frequent visitor, coming to him as a brilliant white light. Enoch dedicated himself to Mauricio when he was a child. For whatever reason, he took an interest in Mauricio at a very early age, and made plans for him. And all though his life, it was Enoch who was there consistently to help Mauricio in life. He was a catalyst for change. He opened Mauricio's eyes to his commitment, and whenever he would stray, Enoch would remind him of his path, sometimes in ways that were not always pleasant. Enoch loved Mauricio, and Mauricio loved him.

Uhr was another cosmic being and biblical figure, who came as a blue light, sometimes translucent, sometimes darker and deeper, always strong. I could feel Uhr's extraordinary devotion to healing. He always came, even when Mauricio doubted he would.

Shallar was the most physical of the light visitors, and appeared mostly in orange and yellow lights. Because of his earthly incarnations and past karmic ties with Mauricio, he too had devoted himself to Mauricio for the purpose of healing. Only Shaller was more insistent with his need to come through. Shaller is a spiritual being, not an ultra-dimensional light being, and lives in the higher astral planes. Throughout his life, Shallar always wanted to merge with Mauricio's physical body and channel through him. Mauricio was never comfortable with what he called "incorporation" and always tried to avoid it. He had seen so many Brasilian spiritists working with lower energies or possessions. These spiritists would incorporate the negative entities into themselves and then release them. Mauricio didn't want to have anything to do with even the suggestion of incorporation. His resistance to Shaller always led to some interesting phenomena.

One night Mauricio asked Marshall if he would attempt to contact his father. Marshall is a direct voice trance medium, and Mauricio trusted his abilities and integrity. Marshall agreed to try it. It was a private sitting, attended only by Patricia, our two friends Emmy and Lenny Chetkin, and me. We all went into the Sanctuary Hall at

Delphi. Mauricio sat between Patricia and Lenny on a small sofa. Marshall sat in his trance chair directly in front of Mauricio. Emmy and I sat on each side of the sofa in high-backed chairs. We were all looking forward to meeting Mauricio's father.

Marshall's control guide is Arthur Ford, the late and well-known medium and spiritual pioneer. It was Arthur who deciphered the famous Harry Houdini code. Arthur acts as a gatekeeper on the other side to protect Marshall and aid in the communication process. Marshall is one of the few direct voice mediums alive today. Once he goes into trance, Arthur enters Marshall's space and uses his voice box to speak. Then you hear Arthur's voice instead of Marshall's. Marshall had channeled Arthur many times before and was looking forward to it that evening, but when Arthur came in, he himself was very uncomfortable. His eyes widened in surprise, and he said, "You've got a different kind of guy here!" Immediately Arthur departed. He didn't want to have anything to do with this channeling session. And when Arthur left, Shaller came in.

The energy in the room was intense. Mauricio recognized Shaller's energy and immediately began to resist. He was afraid that Shaller would use the opportunity once more in an attempt to move into his energy field. Remember that Mauricio didn't want anyone incorporating him, and he knew that Shaller was at it again. As Shaller's energy got stronger, the battle of wills began between him and Mauricio. The tension acted as a catalyst for a vortex of energy to form between Mauricio and Shaller. All of a sudden Mauricio began to levitate, and slowly lifted from the sofa. It was awesome. Patricia and Lenny simultaneously reached up, placed their hands on Mauricio's shoulders and gently pushed him back on the sofa. Mauricio began to lift again. And just as if they had seen people levitating everyday, they reached up again attempting to bring him back down on the sofa. Only this time it didn't work. The energy was so strong that the resistance acted like a springboard and Mauricio went flying across the room and landed in front of a glass table by the door, some fifteen feet away!

Marshall was abruptly jerked out of his trance, and was sitting there looking and feeling groggy. I ran to Mauricio who was lying on his stomach. He looked up sheepishly. He knew exactly what had happened and immediately got up. He gave Marshall a big hug saying, "I am sorry big brother. I fought it. I didn't want Shaller to leave you and slip into me. Are you okay?" Marshall was soaking wet and still recovering from the experience. We all sat around after that talking about it. Mauricio never did get to talk to his father. Patricia and Lenny were laughing. Patricia said it seemed so natural to reach up and bring Mauricio down as he began to levitate, as if she had done it a thousand times. Of course, she hadn't. It was her first experience with levitation.

Patricia and Marshall loved having Mauricio as their guest. He was no ordinary visitor. On another evening we were all in the kitchen preparing dinner. Everyone was helping. We were talking about our upcoming trip to Stonehedge, England, and we were all excited about it. Mauricio was getting something out of the refrigerator, and turned around to say something to Patricia, who was standing in front of the stove. Suddenly we heard a loud "Boom." Something flew across the room and hit the wall in back of the microwave. Startled, we all jumped. What had sailed across the room was a large medallion, about three inches in diameter, which looked like some kind of Mayan coin. Sometimes when he got excited, Mauricio was often a vehicle for apports, items that would materialize out of thin air. We all laughed about it. That evening at dinner every fork bent as we tried to eat. Even though this sounds exceptional, with Mauricio it was commonplace.

Though it sometimes happened when he got excited, phenomena such as apports were much more likely to occur when Mauricio was at ease and not under pressure to perform. When he was comfortable, and with friends he enjoyed, phenomena came through much more easily. During another evening at Patricia and Marshall's house, Mauricio's psychic energy level was really high. He waited until they both left the room, and then he picked up one of their heavy silver forks from the table. He looked at me impishly and held it behind his back, near the base of his spine. When he laid it back down on the table in front of me, the fork had completely curled up and folded over, with only one of its tines left pointing upward. I picked up the fork, which was hot to the touch, and shook it at him, pretending to scold him. "Mauricio," I said, "this energía is for healing, not for making jokes! You should save your power for healing." Mauricio laughed, and with a mischievous look told me "Bobagem," which is the equivalent of "baloney" in English. He took the fork from my hand and stuck the last remaining tine into the cork of the bottle of wine we had just opened. No more than two seconds later the cork, with the fork still in it, flew across the room and landed in the garbage can. I laughed and said, "You see, Mauricio? I speak the truth and the universe is telling you so!" Mauricio just laughed. When Patricia and Marshall came back in, he wouldn't say a word about the fork, he just smiled his most innocent grin.

Although he was usually light-hearted about his gifts, he was keenly aware of the responsibilities that came with them. Throughout his life, Mauricio had often resisted his gift, fearing he would not be able to live up to the weight of its responsibilities. Sometimes when he was feeling heavy with burdens and helpless to change things he would get angry, and shake his fists in the sky at God and the universe for giving him these unusual gifts. "Why me God?" he would ask. "I am no great man, why do you make this for me? Take my gift! Take my vision away! Take it. I want to live my life!"

But even when he felt angry, tired or even disconnected, if there truly was a need Mauricio would always respond. No matter how he felt, if someone was ill or in need, his compassion would always take over. Then he would feel inspired again. I can't remember how many times that happened. No matter what his mood or temperament, he always cared about those who were sick. He was truly a humble man. He had spent years of study and hard work striving to understand and refine his gift, and he was always inventing exercises to increase his level of concentration and focus. He could focus his own energy with incredible accuracy and, in addition to healing, he could use it to accomplish amazing things.

One morning, when we were moving into our little cabana in Georgia, I had filled my Nissan 300ZX with a lot of fragile stuff. Tim, a friend of ours, was in his pick up truck with a load waiting for me to follow. As I backed out of the driveway, I backed right into a ditch. I tried to rock the car, but the left rear tire had fallen into a deep rut and I couldn't get out. Tim came over to look at the problem and gave me the bad news. I would need a tow truck to get the car out.

Mauricio, who had been watching from the doorway, walked over just in time to hear Tim's pronouncement. He looked at the car and he looked at the hole, and he rubbed his chin. Then he said, "No problem. I make this." He walked around to the back of the car and began to focus his energy. Tim just watched in disbelief. I could read his thoughts: there was no way this old man was going to be able to lift that car out of that ditch.

Mauricio was no longer aware of us. He took several deep kundalini breaths, rubbed his hands together very quickly, and said in a

low voice, "energía, energía energía." He then took hold of the
bumper with both hands and lifted the car effortlessly. Mauricio had
raised the back of the car straight up, with me in it, and moved it over
to the left so that the rear wheel was now back on the road. "Okay,"
he said, only slightly out of breath, "we go now." Wiping his hands,
he walked back into the house to get his things as if nothing unusual had happened.

Still in the car, I glanced over and laughed at the look on Tim's
face. His mouth had dropped open and he was staring in disbelief.
You usually only hear stories like this when there is an immediate crisis, and a person acts in an extraordinary fashion. In these situations
people don't have time to think about the impossible, they only act.
Tim didn't say anything. He got back into the truck and followed us
to the new house. Later, when he recovered his composure, he told
everybody what Mauricio had done. My family was impressed, but
since they had seen Mauricio in action many times, this was not particularly surprising to them. It still made Tim nervous though, and
after that day he tended to avoid us. He had a hard time digesting
what he had seen. As my Papa is fond of saying, he didn't have a
drawer to file it in!

Looking back, I can see how Mauricio spurred me into developing
more of my own abilities. He gave me simple exercises that helped
me focus my own energy consistently. One of these exercises involved
sending love and energy to beans to make them grow. The exercise
began with two plates of beans. Every day, five minutes in the morning and for five minutes at night, I would focus on one plate only,
thinking of nothing else but sending love and energy to the beans,
and repeating, "energía, energía, energía." The beans that received
love and "energía" grew two to three times larger than the beans on
the other plate. The same thing would happen when we used plants
instead of beans.

Through exercises like this I learned how to focus my own energy.
Eventually I could bring healing energy through for longer periods
of time, hour after hour, without a break in concentration, just as he
did in his healing ministry. I was an apprentice. It was like being in
school, only a school where I had the undivided attention of a gentle, loving and miraculous teacher.

7

There is no higher religion than human service.
To work for the common good is the
greatest creed.

—Albert Schweitzer

MAURICIO WAS AN exceptional human and spiritual being, who came into the world to express God's love through his gift of healing. One of my greatest rewards with him was experiencing and seeing the miracles of his gifts at work in so many ways. We traveled extensively all over the world, and Mauricio always left a part of himself with each person that he touched.

One day we were asked to work with an eighty-five year-old man who had severe Type II diabetes and was having a very difficult time. His son had brought him to see us and the ailing man didn't know quite what to make of us. He was a Pentecostal minister and Fundamentalist Christian who had been steeped in dogma. This man could listen to other's views on God for hours but, at the end of the day, would not be swayed even a little from his own rigid beliefs. As he lay down on the bed in our hotel room, I could see that he was apprehensive and wondering what to expect.

Mauricio had a sixth sense about people. He sat down in a chair next to the bed, took the man's hand and began to pray, in a way that was familiar and consistent with the man's own religion. Mauricio was careful with his choice of words, and after about five minutes, the man relaxed enough to close his eyes. Mauricio had no intention to bring lights for this man. He wanted to ease him into the experience, and felt the energy by itself was sufficient for the healing. But after ten or fifteen minutes of prayer, he put his hands on the man's head and chest, and two balls of light flashed over the bed.

Despite the man's fundamentalist training, or perhaps because of it, he was deeply impressed by the phenomena and turned out to be very responsive to the healing. Immediately after the session, we could see a change in him. He was quite animated, leaping up from the bed, moving around and acting like a man half his age. He walked out of the room with eyes as big as saucers and said to his son, "Ain't no telling what the Lord's gonna do with that boy!" He was awed by Mauricio's gift, and his very life had been changed. His diabetes came totally under control for almost a year before eventually returning.

I marveled at the instantaneous healings I witnessed. I was in awe each and every time. I loved to see the beauty radiate from these magnificent souls who had just been awakened spiritually. Love had such an impact on them that it changed their whole demeanor. Their bodies stood taller and they had greater confidence. Peace flowed through their eyes, tranquility surrounded them, and most of all, they realized that they too had gifts to share, and love to express from within. Many of them were so deeply moved by what they had experienced that they couldn't help but affect others in their lives in positive ways. It always seemed so simple: just stay in a love vibration and everything else will be okay.

Love is the transformer, the energy of God that lies in each and every one of us. Love has the ability to create profound changes in how we feel, what we think, and how we act. When our hearts awaken, it is only then that we discover all that we truly are and can be here on earth. We see the world differently, and we begin to realize that we can no longer live under the confines of worldly perception. Even our priorities change, and the things that once seemed important no longer have meaning. We realize that we are more than physical beings at the mercy of a merciless world, and we come to know that we are spiritual beings first, who have come to earth to express our own divinity in a human role. When we are in touch with our hearts and the greater power of love, we then feel purpose in everything we do. Mauricio was able to open the hearts of many.

In the U.S., there were many that invited us to come and share Mauricio's gifts with groups of friends and acquaintances. Our travels revolved mostly around Mauricio's healing work and the seminars we taught. We were constantly in demand. Our trips usually lasted four or five days in one place, and then we would move to the next. We usually arrived a day early so that initially we could work with the poor and disadvantaged.

I opened all of the sessions by sharing the knowledge and purpose of Mauricio's lights with the entire group. I gave personal background information about Mauricio, talked about the phenomena of the lights, and I told everyone what they could expect during their energization sessions. I even helped them set their intentions to receive everything they wanted. These introductions allowed them time to relax and prepare for their experience. It was a sacred time, and these were special events. I always finished with a group meditation to set the tone and increase the energy for the healings. One session with Mauricio had the power to change your life.

After the preparation, the people were led into the healing room, sometimes two at a time, sometimes three. Then they would lie down on massage tables, and were told to close their eyes, breath deeply, and relax. Mauricio began the sessions by tuning into their energy. He did this through his breath. He took long, deep, sucking breaths that drew the energy up from his kundalini and through his chakras. The kundalini is the center of the universal core of life force energy located at the base of the spine. As Mauricio breathed, his presence expanded and joined with the person's consciousness, to form an energy field that enveloped them both.

Mauricio always began by rubbing his hands together very briskly, and then gently placing them on the person's head. Then he would lightly touch the person on the left and right shoulders and the left and right sides of the head. He did this to balance the left and right or masculine and feminine sides of the person's energy. He then moved his hands over the person's face, his fingers tracing the bridge of the nose until his middle finger rested upon the third eye, the sixth chakra, the seat of spiritual perception and vision. At the same time, he spoke his mantras in Portuguese to evoke energy, power and harmony. "Energía, força, harmonía, go inside and work," he commanded, "Give spiritual power for my brother and my sister." With these words Mauricio evoked the universal energy of the cosmos to open the person to their own spiritual power. He was literally grasping the energy of the universe, pulling it down out of the sky and up from the ground as he ordered it to work inside of you.

He called these sessions "energizations," and his intention was always the same: to bring whatever love, energy or healing was needed to open a person to their spiritual path and inner guidance. He often said that everyone is at a different point in their lives and only their higher self, the God energy within, knows what they truly need at any given time. Sometimes they needed love to open their hearts to their purpose, sometimes they needed energy for spiritual growth, and sometimes they needed to be healed of a physical problem. Spirit always brought what was needed and Mauricio was the channel through which it flowed. The sheer force of that massive energy moving from the spiritual to the physical, through Mauricio, made the lights flash.

When the lights flashed, Mauricio saw gifts you possessed but hadn't yet discovered, gifts that would fulfill your spiritual potential if accessed and used in this lifetime. He also saw scenes from significant lifetimes and events from the past, and intense or traumatic periods in current and past lives. He could even see your probable future. The lights only flashed for seconds at a time, but those moments often felt like an eternity to Mauricio.

People were told not to open their eyes to see the lights while he was working on them. If they wanted to see the lights, Mauricio would let them know during the session when they could open their eyes. That way they could experience the healing fully without being distracted by the phenomena. Mauricio was sensitive and he always knew while working with you where your attention was. Were you making a connection spiritually? Or were you in your head the whole time thinking about where the light was coming from? It was very important to him that people receive all that he had to give, and not just spend their time looking for the light phenomena, which he felt would diminish their spiritual experience. You could always hear and feel the discouragement in his voice when he spoke about it, and many times it left him wondering if he was misusing his gift.

Still, there was always one in every crowd who was solely attracted to the phenomena. It was his or her only interest. One night, a woman wrote that the only reason she came to the energization was for proof. She wanted to see and then, just maybe, she would believe. Her face had a hard look and her eyes showed little feeling. I smiled at her, knowing she would get her proof soon enough. When it was her turn I watched and waited. She kept her eyes open, watching in disbelief as Mauricio worked. Not only were her eyes open, they were staring. Mauricio was working with three other people next to her in the room, and she followed his every move. Once she even sat up on the table to see what he was doing! It wasn't hard to miss anything. Then Mauricio became distracted. He went over to her and extended his hand in her direction. Two balls of white light shot out from his hand and covered her face with light. It was a beautiful sight, seeing her all lit up like that. The woman immediately stiffened and laid back down. From that point forward, she never opened her eyes again, or moved until it was over. As I helped her out of the room she still felt rigid and was much more tense than she had been when I'd first walked her into the room. I don't know if she received a healing or if even she received the energy. Then again, she had never asked for that. She had only come looking for proof. Well, she certainly got her proof!

While it was important to him that people come for healing and not just for the lights, Mauricio also knew that that one purpose of the light was to attract people who were cynical and suspicious. There were many who didn't believe in God but who were attracted to the lights because they were ready to be awakened to their spiritual purpose and inner faith. According to the Lama Surya Das, "The Buddha did perform certain miracles, but he always instructed his disciples not to demonstrate miraculous powers except to inspire faith in the skeptical…The miracle of Buddhism is a miracle of love, not levitation." Mauricio felt the same way about his lights. During the energization, minds could be opened and healing could occur. Some who came without a shred of religion or spiritual belief in them left with a very strong faith. Others did not become believers immediately, but received the energy that would lead them to faith and healing down the road.

Others just refused to believe, and thought Mauricio was a fraud. These people sometimes exhausted Mauricio's tolerance. He would often stop the session and tell them to leave, that the session was over. Most of the time he wore an open white shirt so people could see he didn't have anything hooked up to his chest. I can remember when we were working with dying patients, and how angry some of them could get. Out of the blue, they would jump off the table in the middle of the session to search for devices on Mauricio. They searched his body, looked under the table, around the room, and everywhere else they could think to look. Mauricio graciously permitted them to do this, and then asked them to leave. It was rare when that happened, but sometimes it did. It was sad to see and for a long time, I did not understand why some reacted like they did.

People didn't realize that when he was bringing the lights for healing, the lights did not come from Mauricio's physical body. They only came through his energy, emanating from his etheric body, the energy field that closely surrounds and envelops the physical body. When the light came through him, it never hurt him. But when the lights would come down into him and enter his physical body, it was very painful. The Light would seer his flesh with symbols of the Christian cross and the Star of David, and he bore these symbols for his entire life. I used a lot of love and vitamin E oil to heal these burn marks. The reason the light would come in this way was to recharge Mauricio's battery. Sometimes it was necessary to help prepare him for his work with sick people. The light would prepare him, and often it would even communicate with him. And there were also times when the light came down to humble Mauricio's ego. Occasionally, when his temper got the best of him, Mauricio would raise his fists to the sky questioning God. The light always gave him an immediate lesson in humility. He was then quick to respond with great respect, not necessarily because he was humbled, but because he understood why things were as they were.

When the lights came to energize and communicate with Mauricio, as they did every year on October 28th, he always tried to make sure he was at the Foundation site. During these "contact" visits, lights entered Mauricio's body to give him instructions, messages that would help him in his life and his healing work. It was almost as if at this time, they were also giving him back the energy he expended through time and his healing work. Sometimes these contacts came more than once a year, and when they did, they also came on the 28th of the month. So Mauricio got into the habit of making the 28th a special day, using it to fast, meditate and go within himself to make his own spiritual connection. I used to call it his spiritual menstruation. I remember once in Brasil, Mauricio was disheartened and disillusioned with his gift, resenting its control over his life. On this particular occasion, he held his fist up to the sky and raged at the lights to leave him alone. Instantly, a bolt of light came from the sky to his fist, knocking Mauricio off his feet, and throwing him nearly fifty feet across the road. It also bloodied the cross stigmata on his chest. It wasn't revenge or anger that drew this light to him, it was Mauricio's own intensity that summoned it in that form. But events like that were rare because Mauricio was one of the most humble and caring men you would ever meet, as well as one of the most human.

When the lights entered Mauricio's physical body in preparation for healing a very sick person, they would come from above him and move through him like lightening rods. They entered through the areas on his body that I refer to as his stigmata-the perfect round marks on his flesh over his chakras, and the shape of a cross over his heart. Although his flesh was actually seared from the energy, Mauricio was totally committed and disregarded the pain. He knew it was a necessary part of the healings. Mauricio and I had been together only a few months when I first saw one of these incidents and it scared me badly. That was the only time I had ever been frozen in place, unable to move, and not knowing what to do.

On that day we were working at Delphi. I was teaching during the day and assisting Mauricio with energizations in the evenings. One of the women in my class, Carol Wendell, had lupus and was gravely ill. She had come to Delphi looking for answers that would either help her get well or ease her transition. She didn't know anything about Mauricio or his healing work. I felt much compassion for Carol and during morning class, I was inspired to ask her if she would accept a healing from Mauricio. Although I had high hopes, I didn't promise her anything. I was only following a hunch. She gratefully accepted the offer.

Mauricio and I meditated together in preparation for her session that evening. After the meditation, I left Mauricio resting on the bed and went downstairs. About ten minutes later, I walked quietly back up the stairs. Just as I was nearing the top, I could hear the hiss of these massive sources of energy popping in unison. It sounded like the stereo was going to explode. When I got to the top of the stairs, I froze to the spot. I saw two large lightning bolts of brilliant white light coming down from the ceiling into Mauricio's forehead and solar plexus. I could even hear the hissing sounds of the energy as it moved into him in a slow, spiraling motion. I was frightened and could only stand there and watch, glued to the floor. I didn't understand what was happening then, and it bothered me a great deal that the energy was searing his flesh. It looked so painful. The five minutes it lasted felt like an eternity.

When it was over, Mauricio tried to get up, but his equilibrium was off and he was having a difficult time. I ran to help and got a mild shock when I touched him. He was one big electrical charge. Everything he tried to touch shocked him or sent out bursts of electricity. I was sure the sound system in the house was going to blow up because it was going crazy, emitting one electrical pop after another. When Mauricio was finally able to maintain a sense of balance, we went downstairs. He placed a cigarette in his mouth, but as he picked up the lighter, a bolt of light came shooting down from the ceiling and flung it across the room, missing me by inches. I was too stunned to speak. I was really shaken. I thought I had already seen all that I was going to see with these lights, but this entire experience was new and totally unexpected.

We got into the car to drive over to Delphi and everything in the car was popping with electricity too. Mauricio couldn't touch anything metal without creating sparks. We arrived at the school and almost immediately he went to work on Carol. The lights that came to assist with her energization were very focused that night. They were intense, concentrated and direct. There was an incredible feeling of love in the room, and it was as if Mauricio and his brother lights were pinpointing the lupus. What an incredible healing! Carol's lupus was cured that night, completely healed, and I knew that she would never be the same. It was then that I realized that the lights that seared Mauricio earlier had been preparing him, augmenting his energy and power for this specific healing.

That night we had also planned to give energizations to the rest of the class, but when we were finished with Carol, Mauricio turned to me and said, "Kimberly, the lights are gone. They don't come back! They have disappeared." He began to breathe and do exercises that would help him, but still no lights came. By then people had gathered and were awaiting their sessions. He told me to go and tell them, "it is not possible, the lights don't come." I told him, "You go tell them!" He said, "No, you go tell", and of course I did. It was humbling to tell them. Naturally the students were disappointed. It was a letdown for them, but they understood the circumstances and appreciated our honesty. But since the class wasn't scheduled to leave immediately, we decided we would simply have to do their sessions the next night. That was a relief for me.

Sometimes, especially after an intense healing like Carol's, the lights really did leave Mauricio. More often than not though, it was Mauricio himself who disconnected. Sometimes after working with large groups, he would be so tired that he would tell me the lights had left him, especially if it was a difficult group and the negative energy was strong. But I knew better. I had seen him give energization after energization even when he was exhausted. At times like these, even when he felt weak and depleted, Mauricio's compassion overruled all other considerations.

There were times when Mauricio was disheartened, especially after working on people who opened their eyes or belittled his work. He sometimes became discouraged, feeling that his work was futile, that he was wasting his time on people whose hearts and minds were closed. It wasn't true. And when Mauricio was inspired again he knew it wasn't true. Everyone who experienced his miraculous gift was touched in some way, manner or form, even if they didn't know it or feel it at that moment. Each time Mauricio invoked the energía, força and harmonía of the universe, God came to give the person on the table whatever energy or healing they could accept at the time. Sometimes it came with lights, sometimes it didn't. Sometimes a healing occurred, sometimes not.

Before we enter into each earth incarnation, we plan our lives and our experiences. We often create lessons that on the surface seem very painful and difficult. But in each of these tests there awaits a gift, a gift of love, given to us for our growth and our soul's development. The difficulty is always looking past the obvious to see the true reason the experience has manifested. And when we are able to see the truth and look past the illusion, we have then begun the process of self-awareness. We should also take heart and know that for every challenge we have created, we have also brought with us the solution. Our free will determines the choices we make.

Each of us is totally responsible for our own lives and everything that happens to us. We are the creators of our own reality. The events that occur in life and the way people treat us are reflections of how we truly feel about and treat ourselves. The Universe always gives us what we want and need, whether we realize it or not. So if we think the world to be an awful place, then the Universe will present situations to us that validate that belief. When we face difficult problems or illnesses in life, we are stretched emotionally and spiritually in order to deal with them. This is how we grow. One can also take solace in knowing that if we are the creators of our lives, we also have the power to change them too. When we experience joy, we must learn to revel in it, to truly bring it into our hearts and into our lives. And we should be careful not to miss all the good things in life because we're too blind or preoccupied to recognize them. When we are able to see the beauty in all things because of God's presence moving through them, then we understand who we truly are. The only reality is the Light of God shining behind and through all things. Everything else is illusion.

Sometimes people aren't truly ready to be healed. Some come into this life with a contract of suffering, to satisfy a previous karmic debt. They have chosen this method to discharge their karma. Others have built their whole lives around pain and struggle, and are afraid or refuse to heal, because it would force them to change how they look at themselves and how they treat others. And there are times when it is not the person's path to be healed, but to prepare for the transition into death. It is during this transition that the opportunities for love and learning occur. Regardless of how it comes, it is in the hands of each person's Higher Self, and it will always happen according to their destiny, not to our desire.

Realizing that each individual's path is a unique one was a difficult lesson for me to learn. At first I thought everyone was supposed to heal, and would want to heal, and I grew up thinking that you could save everyone who needed help. But through my experience in life I learned better.

I remember one night in the hospital in Brasília. Mauricio was bringing through light and healing for an older gentleman. I was holding one hand on the man's heart while the other stroked the air between his heart and his head to create a connection. I could literally see a bridge of light, a bridge of light that was leading him in the distance, very far away. I watched him follow it, walking with a confidence that wasn't like his demeanor at all. He was so very bright. Physically, he looked terrible and in pain, and his face showed despair. And then he just relaxed. After some time he opened his eyes with a gasp, grabbed my hand, and said, "Thank you, thank you, thank you, but I have seen enough and am ready to go." I looked deeply into his eyes. They were filled with anticipation and, at the same time, a look of readiness. I understood exactly what he meant. Although he was not aware of it consciously, he had been holding on. He was ready to cross over, but was afraid to let go because he didn't know where he was going. He didn't have a clue as to what to expect after he died, and it was this uncertainty that kept him holding on. During the healing, he had experienced a bridge of light that had taken him to a place of total comfort and peace. When he saw where he was going, to his new space, he relaxed. He was aware of his light body and the attendant freedom it gave him, and he was no longer afraid of dying.

After he spoke, the man closed his eyes and, within moments, he was gone. I began to cry as I slowly realized that we were never there to save him or cure him at all. Instead we had come to help him with his transition. From that moment forward, I never again felt the need to try to "save" anyone. It wasn't up to me to do that. It's God's will, and the will of the individual soul. Energy flows from Source through the healer when we ask it to come. But what happens afterwards is not the responsibility of the healer, but of the individual. This was a liberating experience for me, because I realized that we are not responsible for the results of any healing. It is "thy will be done" rather than "my will be done."

Less than a year later, this lesson was brought home to me even more completely. A woman phoned Delphi, frantically begging Mauricio and me to come immediately to California to heal her mother who was in critical condition. My gut instinct told me we should go as soon as possible. When we arrived we went directly to the hospital to work with the woman. After one session with her, Mauricio just looked at me. Shaking his head, he told me it wasn't possible to save her, and that it was only a matter of time. I got chills. I felt the truth of it, and I knew the daughter would be devastated. She had so much hope that we could help her mother, and now it was apparent that we had come for other reasons.

During the woman's second healing session, Mauricio and I sensed a celebration in the air. The woman was already in transition, and as her spirit began to leave, we felt an angelic presence come into the room and fill it with serenity. She looked so peaceful and content, smiling the most beautiful smile. It appeared she knew exactly what was going on, and I got the feeling she had somehow orchestrated this event. All I could think of was how brilliant she was to attract people like us who could help her make such a grand exit. I personally couldn't think of a better way to go. What grace! What beauty! What a privilege to be surrounded in love and filled with energy and light as you pass from one dimension to the next. And what an honor to be celebrated spiritually for all that you are, all you have been, and what you will be.

The woman's daughter was devastated and obviously confused. Her intent in calling us had been to heal her mother and prevent her from dying. But it happened so fast! One minute she had hope for her mother's healing, and the next minute her mother was gone. She was terribly upset, and I felt compassion for her. I knew we had done everything we could, and I understood the real reason we had come. She had lived her life fully, and was ready to go. The energy and love that came through gave her the freedom and the vehicle to go in peace.

It took many months for the daughter to come to a full understanding of what had truly happened. She needed time to heal. When
we left, I wasn't sure we would ever hear from her again. But several
months later we received a letter of gratitude and a check for our
expenses. She had come to recognize the beautiful experience her
mother had, and was grateful for this. She realized that the gifts of
light and love we shared had helped make that possible.

8

Experience is not what happens to you, it is
what you do with what happens to you.

–Aldous Huxley

URING OUR TIME together, Mauricio and I spent about
six months of each year traveling in the United States doing
workshops, seminars, and giving energizations. We were
invited by friends, acquaintances, and clients to share Mauricio's healing lights with groups all over the country. We knew these people
through my work in Canada and at Delphi, through Mauricio's previous trips to the U.S., and from the groups we had taken to Brasil

Before we met, Mauricio worked frequently in the United States.
Invited by Anne Marie Bennstrom, he made his first trip here in 1987.
Anne Marie is the owner and Director of The Ashram, a healing center
and health spa in Southern California. She had previously experienced
Mauricio's energizations in Brasil, and had asked him to share his gifts
and experience with her clients at the center. At first he was hesitant and
would not agree to go, because he was a little fearful of traveling to the
U.S. He was uneasy about what could happen to him there. One
evening, not too long after Anne Marie's visit to Brasil, Mauricio was at
the Friburgo, a restaurant and meeting place in Brasilia, socializing with
Joao Carvalho, his best friend and the owner of the restaurant. He was
feeling relaxed, open, and free, and before he knew it, he was on the
telephone accepting Anne Marie's invitation to her center. Mauricio had
only a night and a day to prepare for the trip, and even though he had
reservations about coming to the United States, he was going anyway.

Mauricio had always been intrigued with America, and the similar-
ity of its energy to that of Brasil's. But even though the energy in

both countries was quite intense, it was focused in very different ways. Mauricio saw the U.S. as the counterpart of Brasil. Brasilians accentuate the passion in their lives, often ignoring or disregarding the realities of making a living. On the other hand, Americans are more focused on material things and making money, often to the exclusion of passion, emotion, and personal happiness.

After Mauricio received his airline ticket from Anne Marie, he had second thoughts once more. The notion of working in the United States where capitalism ruled made him nervous. He was afraid that some unscrupulous American would try to exploit his light phenomena for personal profit, or worse that he might be committed to an institution to investigate his power. Adding to his discomfort was the fact that he could not speak or translate English very well, and he really couldn't understand what was being said to him. Fortunately, Mauricio spoke fluent Spanish, and so did Anne Marie. On his initial trips to the U.S., he tried to cover his uneasiness with humor and jokes. Unfortunately, this led some to believe he was not very serious about his work. But there was no one more dedicated to healing than Mauricio. In fact, until he began working at Anne Marie's center, Mauricio had never charged anything for his work. He had never even thought of taking money from those who needed healing in Brasil. It wasn't his custom or the custom of the country for that matter. In the beginning, people made donations, and Anne Marie always took care of him. Later, he began to charge for his work in the U.S., but only as a way to fund his dream, the Enoch Foundation.

Some Americans didn't understand that Mauricio was not looking for fame or fortune. The only reason he accepted any money at all was because he was trying to build a center in Brasil where he could help others. Once, a well-known musician's manager offered him $150,000 to perform a one-night show. Mauricio turned him down cold. On another evening when we were together, the founder of a famous line of hair products offered $5,000 for Mauricio to teach him about the lights. His intention was to acquire this power for himself. I assured him it was not possible and only smiled when he insisted on speaking directly to Mauricio about it. True to form, Mauricio laughed at the mere suggestion.

At Anne Marie's center Mauricio worked on large groups and small groups alike. Sometimes he worked on celebrity clients such as Shirley MacLaine. After many sessions with Mauricio, Shirley devoted an entire chapter of her book *Going Within* to "The Light Man."

It was through Shirley's book that Mauricio met and befriended the well-known spiritual counselor Dr. Wayne Dyer. Wayne had read Shirley's book, but was unconvinced that Mauricio was on the level. "I was intrigued with Mauricio but I also have to admit I wondered whether Shirley had been tricked in some clever way, or even perhaps had 'gone over the edge.' After all, we all know that lights do not speak and act in the way she describes in her book." Nevertheless, when a restaurant owner in Hawaii invited Wayne and his wife, Marcie, to experience Mauricio's healing energies at a gathering at her home, he jumped at the chance to see Mauricio in action. In his book *Real Magic*, Wayne describes their experience:

"Mauricio asked us to follow him upstairs. Marcie and I had decided to do this together so we could corroborate each other's experience and share what we had witnessed together. We lay on the bed diagonally with our heads side by side and held hands the entire time. Mauricio started a cassette player and the room was filled with low-volume mediation music from a flute. He came up behind our heads and placed his fingers on Marcie's forehead. He then spoke loudly the words 'energia, energia, energia' and some words in Portuguese that we could not understand. He removed his fingers from Marcie's forehead and snapped his fingers loudly, repeating 'energia, energia,' again and again. Suddenly, miraculously, the room was literally lit up. Light emanated from his hands and it was as if lightning had struck right in the room. Marcie had her eyes closed but could still see the light through her eyelids. I never once closed my eyes and I was transfixed.

"Then Mauricio touched my forehead with his fingers. His hand was actually very hot. Again, 'energia, energia, energia,' followed by some Portuguese words. I felt as if I'd temporarily gone to another dimension. The light and energy were electrical. My entire body convulsed with enormous shock. The room was aglow. From total darkness to a bright light from this man's hands!

"We stayed in the bedroom for over twenty minutes. During this time, he put his hands on the knee and the ankle of my leg, which I had injured in a bad fall on some slippery rocks the previous week. I felt enormous heat, and the light again emanated from Mauricio and lit up the room. He did this twelve to fifteen times during our session. Then he left the room and walked downstairs drenched with perspiration. Before he left he asked us to stay on the bed for a few moments and let the experience sink in, explaining that we might experience some dizziness.

"We remained on the bed holding hands in silence for several minutes, feeling as close as we'd ever felt in our lives together. We didn't need to speak. Slowly we walked down the stairs together, looking past the other seven or eight people gathered in the room.

"...The next day I noticed that a bothersome growth on the skin of my collarbone, which had been there for several years, was completely gone, and the leg I had injured was no longer sore. In fact, the scabs were almost totally healed over and there was hardly any evidence of the injury.

"...We thanked him and he replied in broken English, 'No, no, no thank me. God's work, not mine.'"

Meeting Wayne and his wife was an honor for me. When I was fifteen years old, my father gave me one of his books to read. He had met Dr. Dyer at a Spiritual Frontier Fellowship conference and was impressed with his philosophy on life. My Dad insisted that I read it. The book was called *Erroneous Zones*. It had an impact on my father's life and he wanted to share it with me, to help guide me in mine. I loved the book and I shared it with several friends.

Mauricio worked with many famous people, such as Dennis Weaver, Jane Fonda, and Liza Minelli. But he was never swayed by their celebrity. All that mattered to Mauricio was helping others. People are people. Some are more sensitive than others. Some are open and some are not. To him, celebrities were just people too, seeking to enrich their own personal experiences in life.

During our travels we were always very selective about the places where we worked. Certain locations were conducive to Mauricio's healing energies, and some were not. Very early in our relationship I learned what to expect. For example, New York City with its intensity made him a little crazy and he had trouble with his energy there. Akron, Ohio, on the other hand, was an ideal place for Mauricio to work. I feel it had something to do with the simple, earthy energy of the Midwest. The name Akron, pronounced Ah-crone by Mauricio, also had a special meaning for him because it is his true spiritual name. It was the name that first attracted him to this city.

Mauricio and I spent the other half of each year in Brasília building the Foundation and bringing tours of Americans to experience the Brasilian healers. The healing culture in Brasil is very different from that in the United States. Although standard medicine is very similar, there are many spiritists and healers in and outside of the cities whom the people swear by and visit regularly. Surgery is performed by these healers, using methods not found in any hospital or university. In fact, many of the healers are illiterate, but have profound abilities and use their healing energies in extraordinary ways. Brasilian healers are devoted to their spiritual ministries too. Many of them work at regular jobs during the day, and do their healing in the late afternoons and evenings. Some of them who I met dedicate three or more days a week to healing. None of them ever charged for their services.

One of the healers that we got to know well is Joao de Luxor da Abadiana. His energy is strong and direct. I saw him heal many with surgery and many without. The night Mauricio first took the boys and me there, João happened to see us waiting in line. He looked at the boys and instructed them to sit and pray with the mediums who were assisting him. I stayed with them because I wasn't sure how long a six and a seven-year-old would be able to sit in prayer without talking or becoming restless. I needn't have worried because Marshall and Patrick responded as if they had done this all the time. They were like little angels. Before I knew it two hours had gone by and none of us had moved a muscle. We were all greatly affected by the powerful energy in the room.

When João performs surgery, he uses a regular kitchen knife to cut, poke and prod inside the bodies of his clients. There is little or no blood, and no one feels any pain even though he never uses anesthesia. Instead he uses mediums. There were at least twenty-five mediums in the room sending ectoplasm, or psychic energy, which creates a natural anesthesia for the patient. In the outer room, additional mediums cleanse the auras and energy fields of the people waiting to see him.

Every night, hundreds line up to see João, calmly waiting in line for their turn. Some people wait for days, often traveling very long distances to receive healing for themselves or their loved ones. I was always amazed at the patience of the people standing in line, considering how impatient we Americans can be if we have to wait more than a few minutes. Several times I saw people who were waiting get turned away. One man, who had been waiting a long time, finally got his turn and stood before João. The medium looked deeply into his eyes and said sternly, "You must forgive your father before I will work with you. Get out of line." The first time I saw that I was shocked, but I later realized just how necessary it could be. If a person will not let go of anger or negative feelings towards another, and these emotions are the source of their problem or illness, they are simply unable to receive healing. I liked this directness. The healers here didn't coddle the people. They were honest and forthright. If they could help you, they would say so. If they couldn't, they told you what to do so that they could.

Mauricio and I brought many groups from the U.S. to visit João. On one trip, Terry Jennings from Hawaii was in front of me. She had just watched the demonstration, and said, "No way, I would never have that done to me. That would really hurt." Since João performs surgery only on some people, I wasn't really worried about her, although she was very frightened. She was going to be next, and she began to pray, pray that he would pass her by. But in the next moment she was facing him, and her eyes were big, evidencing her alarm. Before she knew what was happening, Joao placed his hands upon her head and put her in a calm state to alleviate her fears. She was then led into the surgical area. In just a few minutes, the surgery was completed. Terry was amazed and totally blown away. She looked far different when she came out of the healing room. By the next day the x-like pattern of stitches on her stomach could barely be seen, and by the following night, they were completely gone, leaving no scars. João told her that she would have had serious complications with her female anatomy within the year if the problem were left uncorrected.

Dr. Guedes, who works in Sao Paolo, channels Dr. Fritz. As I mentioned before, he works with long stainless steel needles that he inserts directly into any and all parts of the body, depending upon the affliction. He has the ability to see everything that is going on within a person's energy, and could often prevent illnesses from occurring by healing minor disturbances that are just manifesting in the person's etheric field or energy system. Once when our schedules were crossed up, Mauricio and I brought a group to see Dr. Guedes on the wrong day. He wasn't scheduled to work that day and no mediums were present to send ectoplasm. Mauricio and I looked at each other with alarm. The tour was at its end and we had no more time. We told Dr. Guedes that we had our own mediums, and that they would be able to channel the energy needed to help our group. Almost everyone on our tour was a capable channel of energy, but Dr. Guedes was not satisfied. He was insistent that he could not work without his own mediums. We attempted to convince him for for about thirty minutes without getting anywhere. Let's face it, without the ectoplasm generated by the mediums, those needles could hurt severely. But when Mauricio began to talk about the orphanage and the work that we were doing with children, Dr. Guedes was moved. His heart opened and before we knew what was happening he was going into trance. The group began sending ectoplasm, and everyone got to watch and experience the operations he performed with those needles.

Another woman on the tour was deathly afraid of the needles, certain they would hurt her. I remembered my mother's story and the fear of the needles she had to overcome, and I understood this woman's fear too. She watched as the other twenty-five people in the group went through the experience without discomfort, and she waited until the very last. Wouldn't you know that she was the only one who screamed out in pain? The ectoplasm was weak and that is why the needles hurt her. The group was tired and their concentration had weakened from the last three hours of sending ectoplasm, something they were not used to doing for long periods. But I also feel that she had totally convinced herself that the needles would hurt, no matter what. Her thoughts created her reality. She thought and believed that the needles would be painful, and indeed they were. If one believes things to be a certain way, then they will attract experiences and events to themselves that validate these beliefs. Each of us is the creator of our lives and our reality. If you change your mind, you can change your life. Change your life and you help change our world.

Kate, another woman in the group, had been trying to get pregnant unsuccessfully for two years, but hadn't told Dr. Guedes anything about it. She just let him scan her body to determine what he felt she needed. This time, Dr. Guedes not only used his needles, he also used a knife to make a small incision in her lower back. Kate kept asking the doctor, "Are you finished?" After about an hour when she came out of the recovery room, he gave her a message. Dr. Guedes told her that everything would be okay, and also that she would have what she wanted. She knew exactly what he was talking about, and became very excited as she shared this information with the group. Everyone admired her big stitches and incision for a while. But the next day, something truly phenomenal happened. All of her big stitches had disappeared! What remained were beautiful little artistic stitches sewn closely together, so precise that they would have been the envy of any surgeon. These stitches also disappeared within 48 hours. Kate had wanted her back healed and she wanted a baby. She received both. She became pregnant three weeks after our return from Brasil.

Mauricio was a close friend of Thomas Green Morton, another exceptional Brasilian healer who lives outside of São Paulo, in Pose Allegre. Thomas has the same birthday as Mauricio and was the only other healer in Brasil, and the world for that matter, who possessed the phenomena of lights. Mauricio always said that Thomas' lights had tremendous power, many times stronger than his own. Thomas demonstrated his light phenomena to thousands of people over the years and believed that the demonstration of the phenomena itself was as important as the healing work, because it inspired people to believe in the unknown.

Thomas has a powerful presence that can look and penetrate right through you. He can read your thoughts, and you know that he knows what you're thinking. Thomas's greeting for all people is not hello, but rather the expression "RA!" He says it with such force that you can feel it in your body, and you can't help but respond back, "RA!" RA is the energy of the sun god and Thomas calls out this mantra frequently, not only during his light demonstrations but also to all those he greets.

By the time I met Thomas on one of our trips to Brasil, I felt as if I already knew him. Mauricio had told me many stories of the two of them together, and the events that occurred. I can't tell you how much fun I had sitting hour after hour listening to Thomas and Mauricio speak of their adventures. I remember one of these stories as if I heard it only yesterday:

One night Thomas and Mauricio were driving in the rain from Rio de Janeiro to Minas Gerais. Thomas was sleeping in the back seat and Mauricio was driving very fast, trying to make the trip as short as possible. The roads near Rio are treacherous as they wind through the mountains and, after taking one especially sharp curve too fast, Mauricio noticed something red at his feet. It didn't concern him at first, and he kept on driving. But as the red light intensified, Mauricio became disturbed and called for Thomas to wake up and see the red light. Thomas took one look and told Mauricio to slow down immediately. Mauricio slowed the car, but continued driving. After a few kilometers they came upon a major mudslide caused by the rain. The road was totally blocked with mud, rock and trees. If they had come upon the mudslide going as fast as Mauricio had been driving, he would never have seen it in time. The car would have hit the mudslide and rolled down the side of the mountain, and Thomas and Mauricio would've been killed on impact. It was logical that Thomas was the one to understand the message of the red light. Mauricio had been driving the car, so his awareness was in his mental body. Thomas had been sleeping, and so his awareness was in his astral body. As a result, Thomas was the one who immediately understood that the light was intelligent, and had come to warn them of danger.

Mauricio, Thomas and I talked until the wee hours of the morning. As the evening wore on, the most beautiful patterns began to appear on my white blouse, accompanied by the sweetest, most intoxicating aroma I had ever smelled. As the perfume filled the room, my blouse took on the most incredible designs. It began to look as if it had flowers and clouds of all different shapes all over it. I remember saying to Mauricio, "I will keep this blouse forever!" It was already my favorite white blouse, and I became even more attached to it.

After Thomas left and we were getting ready for bed, I took the blouse off and laid it on the bed. Almost as soon as I put it down, the blouse dematerialized and was gone! I was shocked! How could it disappear? Why would it even want to? I wanted my shirt back! Mauricio laughed at me. I thought that maybe the universe was telling me not to get so attached to material things. But since I wasn't attached to many things, this explanation didn't make much sense. Anyway, I never saw that blouse again.

The next morning we met Patricia and Marshall for breakfast. We were sitting at the table in the hotel restaurant when all of a sudden the table was engulfed with that same strong perfume. Mauricio only smiled and said, "Ah Kimberly, this is Thomas." I knew it was Thomas too. When I had met him, his aura radiated that same sweet smell. Only this was ten times stronger. The scent followed me around for an entire week. It even followed me home to Brasilia. Everywhere I went I smelled it, and even Mauricio was surprised at the duration of this phenomenon.

9

For what is it to die but to stand naked in
the wind and to melt in the sun?
And what is it to cease breathing, but to free
the breath from its restless tides, that it may
rise and expand and seek god unencumbered?

–Kahlil Gibran

IT WAS WELL understood between Mauricio and I that he would be the one to cross over first. From the beginning of our relationship, he warned me that he wouldn't be with me for more than three or four years. He seemed to know when he would be making his transition. I didn't want to hear that and I hated when he said it. Three or four years could go by before you knew it, and in a way it did. These few years were also the longest and most complete of my life. I had been loved. I am loved, and what made it so great is that this love flowed into every avenue of my life. Our love greatly affected those around us. It was advantageous in helping others heal their hearts. It was the kind of love that made you aspire to greater heights, and it was a love that brought me peace and contentment within myself. Whatever that feeling is that makes you look outside of yourself for love was gone. I had always known that if I were truly worthy of love, then this love would find me and last for all eternity. Our time together was precious. The one comforting thought I had was knowing that even though Mauricio may leave me physically, spiritually our cosmic ties would bind us together in our purpose, and he would be there always to serve. I couldn't help but contemplate our destiny. Death in itself can make you feel alone. Does anyone really want to die alone? It sounded bleak when I thought about it. Surely the transition of death is far easier than the experience of birth.

We had just returned to Georgia after seven months in Brasilia, working feverishly to complete our home there and build our school.

We were tired. We had only been home for two weeks, and only God knows why we were being called back to Brasilia so quickly. I only wish I had seen the signs then, but I wasn't looking for them either. Mauricio and I were both in resistance about having to go back so soon, and little did I know the very depth of reason behind that resistance. Ayman was the kind of friend I could rarely say no too. He too had found love and he wanted to share all of those mystical and magical places in Brasil with her. So when he asked us to join them in Brasil, we went without hesitation. I understood his feelings, and it was on our humble land in the jungle where they consecrated their love.

Ayman had always been supportive of our work. He had a strong faith about our project, and being the visionary that he is, he could clearly see the needs of our land. He was willing to help us financially too, and for me, that was a dream come true. It wasn't often we had luck like that. I remember how elated I was that our dream was now becoming a reality.

The beginning of the trip went very smoothly. It was the calmest I could recall. Everything flowed so well, which is highly unusual for Brasil. I wasn't looking for signs, so I wasn't able to see the omens that were speaking to me in so many different ways. I should have seen the signs, but I didn't. Ayman and his love Rowan met us at the airport. We spent the next five days walking the land and intimately sharing the vision of our dream. We showed them exactly what we were doing.

Construction of the Foundation was very frustrating sometimes. Each accomplishment was a major event for us, because it took so long just to complete one thing. It was never easy. It was very difficult to get people to work that far out in the jungle, especially ones who were reliable and wouldn't steal. The Brasilian currency was in flux every day, and as it would sink the price of everything increased. We were consistently working in the United States to support what we were doing here, but at the same time, we were exhausted. We were tired of traveling and working constantly without a break. With Ayman's support we could reduce our travel load and work in a different way than we had before. I was relieved. I was glad we had made the extra effort to come back. It felt almost too good to be true.

Our friends departed, and Mauricio and I decided to spend a few days in Brasília. Although we had been married in the U.S., Mauricio had always insisted that we marry again in Brasil, and he took this opportunity to try and finalize the arrangements. I didn't understand why he wanted to do it, or the urgency of doing it at that particular time. But Mauricio insisted. He said it made for a strong constitution in his country, and that a marriage in Brasil would be recognized more easily. So, we celebrated our love again in Brasília on July 28th. It was amazing to me that in a country where everything seems to take ages, the final arrangements for our marriage ceremony could fall so easily into place in just two short days. Once again the signs were speaking to me, but I didn't hear them.

To be married in Brasilia was a very casual affair. It wasn't a big deal. You had to go to court and sit in an open room with others who were getting married on that day too. When your names were called, you and your witnesses would stand before the Judge and go through a somewhat professional civil ceremony. There was nothing really romantic about it, but we made it special. The day of the ceremony was also special to us. The twenty-eighth was our day, and it was on the twenty-eighth day of each month that Mauricio always had a very strong contact with the lights.

During these times, Mauricio was also very sensitive, sometimes overly sensitive. His power was often sporadic, and it was during this time that the phenomena were especially strong. My menstrual cycle was also like clockwork, and since the day I stopped breastfeeding my son Patrick, my period has always begun on the twenty-eighth of each month. Except for this time. It was another sign I didn't get, another omen I didn't see. Why should I have tried to put some great meaning into something as simple as missing my menstrual cycle? The truth is I could usually see everything, and would always respond to the subtle messages the universe was giving me. Normally I listen for the signs and then rely on my intuition to guide me. I look at everything in our world as a reflection of myself, and it always tells me how I am doing in life. The universe speaks to us in many languages. And if we are sensitive, and follow our hearts, the direction we need to take will be there, and we will be guided. But on this day things were different.

I awoke at dawn the following morning with the strangest feeling, one I couldn't shake. I lay there in the bed for a long time, listening to the parrots sing their lovely song. There was a cool breeze that morning and the air was brisk. It was always like that in the early morning hours in the jungle at this time of year. I was reflecting again how smoothly everything had gone, but still, there was something unusual lingering in the air. I felt an uneasiness, but I just couldn't put my finger on it. I didn't know why, but I told Mauricio that we would sleep at a hotel in Brasília that night rather than returning to the Foundation. It seemed like a good idea to him at the time too.

We had a lot to get done that day. I was tickled we were leaving Brasilia a day early because everything had flowed so well on our trip. We had a late lunch that day. Since we both hadn't eaten anything, we went to one of our favorite restaurants. After we had finished eating, Mauricio complained a little about his equilibrium. He was feeling a little nauseous but not in the sense of throwing up. He broke out into a cold sweat, and for a minute we even thought it might have something to do with the food he ate. I told Mauricio that I would postpone our meeting with the lawyer until the next morning, and that I would take him to the hotel immediately to rest.

We weren't in our hotel room for even a minute before Mauricio screamed out in pain. Because of his high tolerance for pain, I knew at once that this was serious. He immediately lay down on the bed and tried to control his breathing. And I could see that he was hurting badly. I called the hotel doctor who came quickly. He checked Mauricio and tried to diagnose him, but he really couldn't tell what was wrong. Since he couldn't find anything, the doctor didn't think it was serious. But I knew differently. I knew how much pain Mauricio could stand, the doctor didn't. I took command and insisted in my pigeon Portuguese that he get us to the hospital. Mauricio was growing progressively worse and finally, after what felt like an eternity, the ambulance arrived.

From that moment on, things happened very quickly and it was all like a blur to me. I was afraid and feeling somewhat helpless, but I certainly wasn't going to act like it. My love needed to see my strength, not my fear. The ambulance took Mauricio to the doctor's own clinic where they gave him tests, and then left us alone in the room for a while. Mauricio lay there on the doctor's table. He didn't look good. I was holding his hand sending him my comfort as best I could when suddenly he sat up perfectly straight and looked at me. His eyes were searching mine. I composed myself to look strong and at ease for him, even though I was scared. The love in his eyes could speak a thousand phrases. He didn't need to say anything, but he did. Oh, my God, I realized, he was saying goodbye. He said, "Oh, my love, it's time I go. I make promise to you I would say good-bye. I love you muito, muito, muito. Eu tiamo muito. You will always be my bell, the sound of the universe. Don't worry about Marshall and

Patrick. I will watch over them. I love Marshall. I love Patrick. I love all my children. I make big protection for you forever. I will be close and I will help much more on the spiritual plane because I will be free of this body. Don't worry my love. We will always be together. I will never be far. We have work to do. You are my Neika, and you will always be my Neika."

I began to cry. This was the moment I had never wanted to face. We were actually saying good-bye, and it didn't seem fair. It was all too fast. I needed more time. He fell back down on the table. As he lay there my head began to spin. The ache in my heart was now throbbing with a deep pain, as if it were slowly being ripped from my chest. All I could think was that he was going now, and that it was all over. We had said our good-byes, and that was it? Surely, our parting would have more substance than that. Not just one brief moment to speak our undying love. And it did. God bestowed upon us a little more time. Mauricio didn't go.

The doctor came into the room to say that Mauricio had had a heart attack and we needed to move him to a hospital for proper care. I had to move quickly because I wasn't about to trust him to a regular hospital in Brasília. I needed to find a private one. I didn't know much about the hospitals here, except for the two big public hospitals where Mauricio and I did healings. I was sure that I didn't want to bring him there. I knew his problem was delicate. He needed special care. This was an absolute knowing that I had.

Finding a good hospital turned out to be a little more difficult than I imagined. It was hard to find a room in a private hospital in a city with limited space and resources on a moment's notice. With the doctors help I finally found a private clinic with the facilities he needed. So off we went in another ambulance to the Clinica Daher. I didn't think we were going to make it. Mauricio had the dry heaves. He kept reaching for his chest and at times he would cry out in pain asking me to be near to him. "Don't be far, my Love", he whispered. It was so difficult for him to breathe. I could feel his pain, and still all he could think about was me.

We admitted Mauricio to intensive care. The hospital staff was having a great deal of trouble stabilizing him. They wouldn't let me come into the room for a while because of all of the things that they had to do to help him become stable. I sat outside the door for what seemed like an eternity, in a little room outside of the ICU, staring at the cold beige floor. This neutral color seemed to be everywhere in this small hospital. There was nothing remotely glamorous about the place, though it was clean and simple.

An hour and a half had passed before they called me in. I remember walking in, pushing my way through the two big metal doors. I entered a big room that could have accommodated three or four patients. Mauricio was the only one there. There were no curtains separating the beds, and if there was a window, I never saw it. They had finally gotten Mauricio stabilized. He didn't seem to be in so much pain anymore, and his breathing was less erratic. I was just so darn happy to be back in the room with him. He smiled weakly at my presence. Our embrace was tender, and when I held him, I could feel how fragile he truly was.

I had only been in the room a few hours when another doctor came in and told me that I would have to leave soon. But, where was I to go? I certainly wasn't going to drive two hours back to the Foundation, and do what? Pace? Worry? Or was I to go back to the hotel, and do what? More of the same? There was nowhere else I wanted to be. I wanted to stay with the man that I had grown to know and love so deeply. Our love was as fresh and pure that day as it was in the beginning when I took him into my heart. We had discovered the depths of each other's souls and we would carry that with us forever.

In my broken Portuguese, I told them I wasn't leaving. Tears pouring down my cheeks, I told them it would take the police to carry me out. I knew the walls that now contained me would be my home for as long as necessary. They were insistent about those rules-I simply could not stay. I guess it was no different from the rules and regulations in America. My perception of Brasil felt diluted. I always thought it to be a free country where most people, and I mean this in a good sense, express what they feel and do what they want to do, within reason. Mauricio heard them trying to make me go and his heartbeat became erratic again. He weakly cried out, "She don't leave. She don't go. If she go, I go." Between the threat to his heart and my emotional outbursts, they clearly saw they were going to have to break the rules. So, they let me stay, but with great reluctance.

I sat there, watching Mauricio all night long. Watching and waiting with the doctor who was monitoring him. At 2:00 a.m., Mauricio was completely stabilized and the doctor again asked me to leave. He said I needed to rest, but I was afraid to go. I was sure that if I left, or even went to sleep, Mauricio could go without me there. I didn't so much have a problem with him going. I always knew this day would come. Mauricio had told me so. I just wanted to be there for him, and for me. And I had to be awake and aware when it happened. I wanted to be in the room when he left to enter his new space. I had to feel it. Surely, God would grant me this one wish?

The next morning Mauricio was doing a little better and I had hope. But the anxiety of not being able to communicate completely with the staff, or understand exactly what was going on technically was tearing me apart. I felt so alone. I stepped out of the room to call home where Susan, our nanny, was with the children. I told Susan what had happened, and to call my mom and papa who were in New York giving a workshop, and to ask them to please come right away.

I had not eaten, slept or changed clothes in more than twenty-four hours. And since Mauricio was feeling a bit better, I hurried to the hotel to shower. I was gone an hour at the most. I raced back to the hospital. My love was still there. In crisis, your fears and thoughts can sometimes get the best of you at crucial moments. Sometimes you think the worst, rather than trusting that through your intentions, all of your wishes and dreams will come true. "Thank You, God!" I thought. Mauricio even looked a little better. But in that short time, Mauricio had become preoccupied and worried about me. I assured him that I was strong and fine. I knew that if he didn't feel my strength, he would have a much more difficult time. So I sat by his bedside and projected my strength into the room and into him.

As I sat in the chair watching Mauricio I soon became very sullen. I began to think about our Brasilian wedding ceremony only two days before. It seemed so odd. It was then I began to think about all of the signs and the omens that had been speaking to me for the past ten days. I was beginning to understand why Mauricio had pushed me so hard to get married in Brasil. Intuitively he knew he was going to go soon. He wanted to be sure that I was legally his wife there too, so as to avoid any legal problems. Wasn't that just like my Mauricio? Staring his own death in the face, his only concern was for me. He had one of the purest hearts I ever felt. Truly this was a man with a heart of gold. I was devastated at the thought of losing him, having only found him a few years before. Going on without him would be difficult, but I knew his love would be there and the memory of that love would always continue to live.

We talked a lot as he drifted in and out. I spent the rest of the day just gazing at him, helping him whenever I could. I still hadn't slept.

I sat in my chair and watched Mauricio go in and out of consciousness, calling for me whenever he awoke. At least I was there for him, and able to give him some comfort. The staff of the hospital wasn't sure whether they liked me or not. After all, who was I to break their rules? They didn't know us from Adam. But I couldn't complain. They let me stay without any further arguments.

That evening, an English-speaking doctor was assigned to Mauricio. Finally, I could communicate! The doctor told me that Mauricio's life was in danger, and that the only hope for his survival was a heart operation. For that, we would have to fly him to São Paulo. But the doctor said that we couldn't even think about moving him until he was stable, and he hoped that by Monday Mauricio would be well enough to make the trip.

All of his life, Mauricio had been terribly afraid of anything that had to do with his heart. His father had died after a heart operation and Mauricio was sure that if he ever had heart surgery, he too would die. But we didn't have any options. According to the doctor, surgery was our only one. The doctor left the decision in my hands. Since Mauricio could not be moved immediately and there wasn't anything we could do at the moment, I decided I would wait to make the decision. I didn't have to think about it until later.

The next morning I was relieved to hear that Patricia and Marshall were on their way. They were driving home from New York for a quick change of clothes before racing to Miami to catch a flight south. Even if they managed to get a flight on such short notice, it would take them at least twenty-four hours to reach us, because there were no direct flights to Brasília. When I told Mauricio that they were coming, tears fell from his eyes. He was deeply touched and most happy that I would have someone there with me. This gave him a peace. I only realized later that he was holding on for me. Although his pain was great, it was not so great for him to overlook the fact that he was leaving me alone in this foreign land. It was a selfless act of true love, one that will affect me for the rest of my life.

That night the hospital staff actually brought me a cot to sleep on. It had taken two days of watching how strong our love and my determination were, but they finally relented. They even decided they liked us and began to treat me warmly and with great care. I still sat up in the chair all night, watching and waiting for something to happen. I just knew that if I fell asleep he would go and we wouldn't have that one last moment together that I so desperately wanted. Still, I must have dozed off because somehow during the night, when a nurse was checking Mauricio, she slipped off his wedding ring and took it from his finger. I never saw a thing, but when Mauricio awoke the next morning, it was the first thing he noticed. He cried for his ring, and I became very upset. How could someone do such a thing? Who would do that? How could that have happened? I didn't act rationally.

I jumped up and quickly called a taxi to take me to a nearby store so I could replace the ring. In typical Brasilian fashion, this became a problem. Stores didn't normally keep merchandise on hand and I ended up having to custom order one made especially for him. When I returned, Mauricio was doing much better, at least in spirit. He bugged me about running off to the plaza to get some ring. "Ah, Kimberly, voce te maluca!" He said, "You are crazy. You should know it's not possible to go in the store and just buy a ring. It is not the custom. You don't eat. You don't sleep, my love. You need to have care. Rest here with me." Smiling and feeling tender hearted for him, I assured him that I didn't drive to the store, as if that made a difference. As I sat with him, we stared into each other's eyes, telepathically acknowledging each other's thoughts.

Mauricio kept drifting in and out throughout the day. But in between, we laughed and joked, and felt the tenderness of our love. We spent the rest of the day and night talking about our love and life together. But Mauricio was not getting better. He kept having setbacks, and although he made it through another day, I was still feeling a great deal of anxiety and uncertainty. I was also unsure about whether to authorize the surgery or not. I didn't let on to the doctors that it was even an issue, but I knew how resistant Mauricio was to the idea. He was my first priority, and I was not about to go against his wishes. Again, it was in the hands of fate.

The morning of Sunday, August 1 felt very strange. Everything was electric, energized. I might have even been a little out of it. By that time I was pretty worn out, and my physical senses were numb. Yet my spiritual self felt fully awake. Mauricio was feeling it too. The staff had to give him something stronger for his pain. His breathing had become more difficult with each passing day, and the pain in his chest was only getting worse. That morning he looked so tranquil. There was a peace about him. He drifted in and out, and when he was in, again he spoke his words of love, and I spoke mine.

By then, I had come to grips with the fact that he was holding on for me. His suffering was more than I could stand. I could see how hard it was for him to breathe, and it was beyond my understanding how he could endure the kind of pain I could see he was feeling. I told him that I knew it was time, and it was okay. I told him to let go. We had had our special time together, and that meant everything. I told him not to worry. Mommy and Papa were coming, and I wouldn't be alone. I told him to be at peace. I stroked his hair and rubbed his head and told him with a smile that I would love him forever, no matter what happened. How I admired him, lying there enduring the pain, his only focus to love and protect me.

In the early afternoon he seemed especially serene. I watched him drift off and I could tell he was not in his body. He was traveling. I knew he was. He looked so free. Where was he? What was he seeing? What was he doing? At that moment, my Mom and Papa were just turning from the main street in Blue Ridge, Georgia toward the highway that would take them to the Atlanta airport. As Marshall made the turn, Patricia felt a tremendous energy course through her like a powerful wave, sweeping from the top of her head to the soles of her feet. It was how she experienced Mauricio when he was giving her Energization. Then she saw Mauricio, just for a moment, looking straight into her eyes. "Good-bye," he told her. Patricia began to cry. She said, "Marshall, Mauricio just came. He's leaving and he says 'good-bye.'" They were heartbroken. Until that moment, Patricia and Marshall had hoped that Mauricio would recover. But with this message, they knew he was going and that they would not arrive in time.

My Mom and Papa had a special relationship with Mauricio. They were cosmic brothers. It was more than a friendship. It was a cosmic relationship. We were all best friends and shared a common purpose. We traveled everywhere together in work and in play. Mauricio used to say, "Marshall, you are my cosmic brother." And with a twinkle in his eye he would look at my mom and laugh and say, "and you are my Mommy," even though he was years older than she was. He loved them dearly, and he felt their integrity, sense of purpose and dedication to healing.

Back at the hospital, another doctor came to check on Mauricio and to tell me they had scheduled the surgery in São Paulo for the next day. By that time, I had already mentioned it to Mauricio, and I could see how uncomfortable he was with even the thought of it. Still, all I could think of was that we would cross that bridge when it was time. I knew we were in the hands of destiny. It was only several hours later when my love had yet another small heart attack and other respiratory problems. They put tubes down into his lungs. His breath was no longer his.

At exactly 7:50 p.m. on that bleak Sunday night, Mauricio left me, and all of those that loved him. There I stood over him, afraid to make a move or a sound. I was afraid to cry for fear they would make me leave him in this room. It all happened so quickly. All I wanted was just one last moment to say goodbye as he was leaving. I spoke gently in his ear of my undying love. The tone of my voice assured him of the freedom that I longed for him to feel. I couldn't stop stroking his beautiful fine white hair, the hair I would never run my fingers through again. I kissed him over and over as I told him that our love would always be alive, that I would share his spirit with many, with all of those who cared to know. The depth of his life and love was meant to be shared. And I, for a moment, honored this gentle man's existence and the life that he lived. We had made a promise to each other, and this promise eventually would become my destiny.

His spirit was leaving his body now, slowly but surely. My own body was full of tingles. My emotions were unlike any feelings I had ever felt before. Experiencing a transition of death is incredible. I could see his brilliant golden white light lifting from his body. Words can't begin to describe the beauty I saw in this golden light. I kept talking to him, telling him good-bye over and over, and that it was okay for him to go, that my only wish was for him to be free and happy. "You have made your mark in life, my love," I said.

For forty minutes I had invisible walls around me. No one came close. How was it possible, that once somebody dies, they don't immediately begin their procedures? At 8:30 on the dot, the walls came down and I was now very aware of people moving slowly towards me. It felt like everything was in slow motion, and I began to tremble. My body slowly went into convulsions. I was already in a trance-like state from the last four days. I was lucid, able to see the invisible energies so clearly. I was not in any condition to go anywhere or do anything at that moment. They brought me to a chair. I could barely walk. My physical condition must have been much weaker than I realized. They fed me a pill that I found out later was a Valium. I must have looked like I was shattered and in shock. The nurse was watching me closely. But I couldn't take my eyes off of Mauricio as I watched him go.

I looked up and saw his spirit actually turn around. He turned back and hovered over me. I felt him smile. I saw his huge, warm, golden energy, and he filled me with immense love. Then he passed through me with an energy so powerful that it stilled me instantly from the convulsions. I was mesmerized by the energy and captured by the moment. I breathed deeply for a few minutes until he moved away. And then suddenly, I was completely alone.

The Man of Light, my Mauricio, at his Contact Point in Brazil.

Mauricio with television star Dennis Weaver.

Mauricio, actress-visionary Shirley MacLaine and friends.

My sons, Marshall and Patrick, at the
Foundation Enoch in Brazil.

Marshall, Patrick and I with orphaned
children we worked with.

The late Robert Monroe, founder of the Monroe Institute, a pioneer in the exploration of human consciousness; with Mauricio and I.

My stepfather, Papa Marshall, Mauricio and my mother Patricia

Mauricio's stigmata.

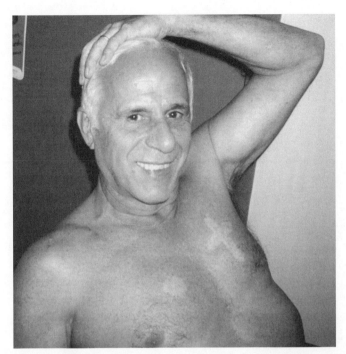

Stigmata over Mauricio's chakras and cross stigmata.

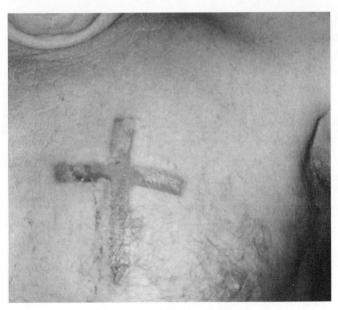

Close up of cross stigmata.

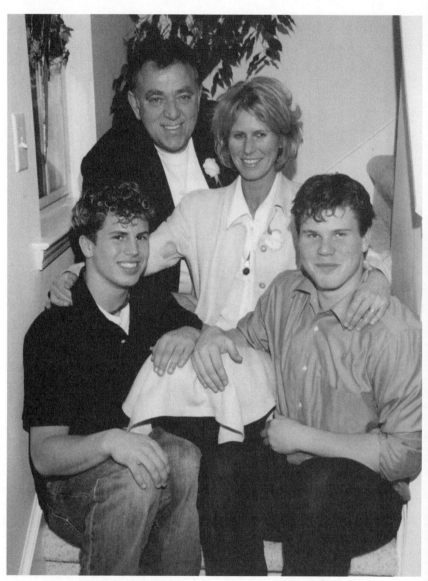

Kimberly and Charles, Marshall and Patrick

10

...and we ourselves shall be loved for awhile
and forgotten. But the love will have been
enough: all those impulses of love returned to
the love that made them. Even memory is not
necessary for love. There is a land of the living
and a land of the dead, and the bridge is love,
the only survival, the only meaning.

—Thorton Wilder

THE HOSPITAL WOULD not permit me to leave. They knew I couldn't drive in my condition and insisted that I stay and rest longer. I was a mess. It was only after I sat down in the chair that I noticed the blood that had begun to flow. How synchronistic and yet appropriate. I thought of the omen and what it meant to me. A menstrual cycle is renewal, a clearing away of the old to make way for the new. My menstrual cycle had begun to flow heavily, and it was a signal to me that my former life was ending to make way for the new life that was beginning. I needed to go back to the hotel so that I could change my clothes and bring Mauricio's clothes back. We had only brought one outfit each on this trip, as we were only staying in Brasilia for the night. I was happy that I had packed his favorite clothes, for it was these clothes that he would wear at his viewing. And I was glad that I would bury him in the casual clothes that he liked so much. He wouldn't have wanted to see his body in a stiff suit.

There were many decisions that had to be made. In Brasil, it is a law that the dead must be buried within twenty-four hours. There was little time to make elaborate arrangements, and a viewing and burial has to be prepared very quickly. The quick decisions I had to make brought me back to a harsh reality, for I had to review and sign many documents, make funeral arrangements, decide on the burial, and worst of all tell Mauricio's family,

The thought of having to call home to tell my children that their papa had passed on was even worse. He was their father in every sense of the word, and they had come to love him deeply. It had only been

101

a few days since we told them how happy we were to be coming home early, and not to worry because we would be back in Georgia very soon. It all seemed so surreal and shocking at the same time. So much had happened so quickly. In a moment our world had changed. I knew I had to be strong for Marshall and Patrick when I called. I prepared to tell them in the most loving and wisest way I knew. I needed to be clear, and make some sense out of the situation.

How do you tell your children that their Papa is gone? I told them everything that had happened, and that Mauricio said that he loved them very much. I also told them how he said goodbye and that he promised he would be with them always. It was all such a blur at that point. One thing was certain; they didn't understand the finality of my call. They really didn't comprehend the true impact of what had happened, nor did they understand why they were leaving Georgia so suddenly to return to Brasil. But since they were coming to be with me, they wanted very much to come. I felt strongly in my heart my place was here in Brasil. My purpose was here too. I had built a life with Mauricio and I could not abandon it now under any circumstances. What other choice did I have but to put my children on an airplane and fly them down to be with me? We had made a home in Brasil, and Brasil was where we would stay.

In Brasil, Mauricio and I had very few friends. He knew a lot of people, but there were few with whom we were intimate. Ronaldo Pacheco was our lawyer. Although he hadn't known us for very long, he was there to help as soon as he heard the news. Ronaldo was selfless in every way. He had a good heart, and he helped me through the entire ordeal. He was a knight in shining armor to me.

João de Carvalho, owner of the Friburgo, and his wife Luzia were two of our best friends. The Friburgo is a modest bar and restaurant with a small deli-market in Brasília. That is where I met Joao. The Friburgo was Mauricio's favorite hangout for years, despite the fact that João hid the silverware every time Mauricio came in. João always good-naturedly tried to make Mauricio use plastic utensils, because he was tired of buying new forks, knives, and spoons to replace the ones that Mauricio bent, melted or curled. There was a time when Mauricio was very popular there. Sometimes the people would come just to see Mauricio's phenomena, and that made the restaurant even more popular. The people were always curious and loved Mauricio's good nature and sense of humor. It wasn't often that someone took note of what Mauricio was really feeling underneath. There were few that could see the concerns that Mauricio carried with him in his life and for the world. Joao was this kind of friend. He knew Mauricio's heart well, and I knew his love for Mauricio was genuine. After Mauricio crossed over, João and Luzia helped take care of me too. I am still so very grateful to them for taking charge of and dealing with all of my everyday tasks. They handled so many things for us. It gave me the time to grieve. The people of Brasil are like that. Once they love you, they become your family, and you become a part of them for life.

Ruth de Oliveria, a director of the Bank of Boston, was our banker, and also our good friend. She was the only person in Brasilia that I could speak with in English, and I got to know her well. Much of what I learned about Brasil, and how things worked there came from her. She was a true friend, someone I could trust. Although August 1st, the day of Mauricio's death, was her birthday, Ruth left her party immediately to help me. It was kind of ironic. She started out the evening celebrating her birth, and now here she was with me during the transition of Mauricio's death.

Ruth was my angel. In the final hour of that night she put me to sleep tucked safely away in a hospital bed. At that point, I was feeling privileged. They gave me a private room with a shower. It was difficult to sleep well that night. I was crampy and restless from being overtired. They tried to give me another sedative, but I wouldn't take it. I was out of it enough already. It had already been one of the longest nights of my life, and I drifted in and out. I could only lie there and contemplate thoughts of Mauricio. I was missing him already. I knew he was close, but that didn't make it any easier. Feeling his presence did help though, and with the strength of his love, I was able to get through the night.

The following day we held an all-day viewing of the body, attended by family members and many of the people who had known Mauricio in Brasil: colleagues from the Federal Policía, friends from the Tribunal and the University of Brasília. Mauricio's body was buried in Juiz de Fora, the city in which he was raised. His grave rests alongside those of his mother and father.

The next day, Ronaldo drove me to pick up Patricia and Marshall from the airport. By the time the funeral was over, my voice was completely gone. I couldn't say much to them, but I didn't have to. They understood and responded to me moment to moment. They displayed a selflessness and I felt their deep and unconditional love. With each step, they helped me to go on.

That night I lay down to sleep for what I felt would be an endless night. I was exhausted, still unable to sleep from being over-tired. The dryness in my throat made me even more aware of the ache in my heart, and I lay there in the dark full of many thoughts. Memories would pour through me in an instant and then just as quickly they would disappear. As I tossed and turned, I was suddenly inspired to get up and call Thomas Green Morton to tell him about Mauricio. Thomas has a charismatic presence. He didn't have to say a word for you to feel his power. It not only came through his eyes, but from his whole demeanor. Thomas was saddened by the news and was filled with compassion. As he so often does, in his commanding voice he said to me "RA!" "Come, now, I will help you!" The news didn't seem to surprise him though, and it made me wonder what he thought about Mauricio's sudden departure. Although knowing Thomas, he may already have had a premonition of Mauricio's death before it happened. After all, their relationship was beyond anything one would consider normal. They were unique together and were quite a pair. They shared a knowledge of powers that were, in many cases, inexplicable to the human mind. And whenever the two of them came together, they could do things that neither could do alone. The demonstration of their combined power always left me in awe.

I raced down the hall of the hotel to tell Patricia and Marshall about our impending trip to Sao Paulo the next day to see Thomas. It wasn't easy, but in my raspy voice I managed to tell them of my urgent need to see him. They saw the determination in my eyes and responded to me, "Sure, Kimberly, okay, tomorrow we will go." They accepted my request without question, hugged me, and urged me to get some rest.

I felt a great deal of anticipation about our upcoming meeting. What was in store for me there, and why did I feel the need to suddenly fly off to Sao Paulo and see Thomas? What was I thinking? Did I think that Mauricio would appear to me through Thomas? Did I think I would be that much closer to my love? Was I searching for resolution? What was there about his death that was left to resolve? I didn't know much of anything, except that it was comforting to know that I would be received by someone like Thomas, someone who knew Mauricio's gift so well. I was sure he would have something significant to say to me, and I convinced myself that I was not acting irrationally.

The next day we flew to São Paulo and took a taxi to Thomas's home in Poso Allegre. Marshall sat in front with the driver, and my mother and I sat in the back. We were all exhausted. Patricia and Marshall were drained from worry, and were tired from the three days of travel. I was just plain worn out. We intended to use the four-hour taxi ride to rest, and after an hour or so, Patricia and Marshall fell asleep. I was sitting with my face to the window, eyes closed, praying for inner strength. Soon after, waves of love began to wash over my body. I felt it from within and all over me. I felt its soft caress ease my grief, giving me a deep feeling of peace. For the first time since Mauricio left, my mind relaxed totally and I felt okay.

Memories of Mauricio's healing touch and how he selflessly helped others came flooding into my mind. A few years back my mother had pulled her sciatic nerve very badly while moving furniture. I had never seen her in such pain. No one could help her, not even the painkillers she was taking. The doctor told her to lie on her back and rest, that there was nothing he could do. Her chiropractor drove two hours from Atlanta to see her, but he couldn't help either. Only time could heal the nerve and that could take months, maybe even years. Papa and I did everything we could think of to ease her misery, but for three solid days we watched her suffer in terrible pain.

Mauricio had been in Brasília during this time, one of the few times we were apart. But he was flying back that night. I picked him up at the airport, and although it was almost two in the morning when we arrived at their home, Mauricio went to work on my mother immediately. He placed her on the edge of the bed with her back facing towards him. He was kneeling on the floor when he took his right hand and placed it over the problem area. He then moved his hand back and forth, every so often pulling the energy and then throwing it out. He was extremely focused and he was sweating profusely. He didn't even realize that we were there. As we watched, I knew that this healing was more unusual than any other healing I had ever seen him do. He made sounds I had not heard before, and the healing itself was much more physical. It reminded me of how the shamans work. He just kept pulling and pulling the energy out, which lasted about an hour. There were no lights this time, just intense energy. I was in awe. When he was finished my mother's pain was completely gone. I knew the severity of it, and I couldn't believe it. Mauricio told her that she would be walking in three days. And just as he said, my Mom was out of bed three days later. But on the following day, I could see that Mauricio was now carrying the pain of her sciatica in his own body. It took him two weeks to walk it all out.

I asked him how he did that? How did you heal her so quickly? Mauricio told me he pulled all of the pain energy out so that the body could shift back naturally to where it's supposed to be, and the nerves could then heal. He explained that the body has a more difficult time healing when it is in pain. For example, if a dying person is in severe pain, the pain can hold you in your body and prevent you from dying. I understood what he was saying.

I was moved to the depths of my soul at the level of caring of which this man was capable. And it wasn't just family who he cared deeply about. Mauricio unselfishly gave of his gift to everyone who needed it. Once, a frantic friend called the wife of one of the Delphi staff with news that her brother had overdosed and was in the hospital in critical condition. They didn't think he would make it, and she didn't know where to turn. The woman was told that there was someone who might be able to help. Although she didn't know us very well, she called to ask if Mauricio and I would go to the hospital to do a healing on him. We weren't sure about going at first. The people at the Fannin County hospital were not used to people like us, and I didn't know how well we would be received. But Mauricio had a good feeling about it, and decided we would go.

The man we had come to see was in the intensive care unit. His sister and the duty nurse left us alone in his room. Mauricio stood at the foot of the bed calling his brother lights, while I stood with my hand on the man's heart sending him love and telepathically calling him back to his body. After some time, three lights appeared and sparked over the man. Although he was unconscious, he smiled. And then his smile got even bigger. Suddenly he realized he wasn't leaving, but was coming back, and I was not the angel of death after all. This was just the opposite of what he had expected. As he came back into full awareness, his body thrashed on the bed. He awakened, angry to be back in a world he was desperately trying to leave. He looked so helpless lying there, and I felt compassion for him. The man's anger had no affect on Mauricio who was calm and understanding. He knew that he had brought this man back to his awareness and back into his body. That was all he had ever intended. The man had healed, and was taken out of Intensive Care that evening. We heard later that the man had turned to God and had become very religious. He even shared parables out of the bible with anyone who was willing to listen.

My awareness returned slowly from this memory, and I was back in the taxi on the way to Thomas's house. I was still facing the window with my eyes closed, and I was trying to sleep, but I was too restless from the visions, from all the pictures in my mind. Then out of the clear blue, out of nowhere, I saw one of the clearest visions I have ever seen. There was my Papa, Marshall, standing just outside the window of the moving taxi, staring back at me! His eyes were so soft, yet they pierced my own eyes with an incredible love. I could feel it flowing from him into me. I was being filled with it. Marshall was so beautiful standing there, sending me waves of love and telling me everything would be okay. I was totally captivated by this vision and the feeling I was receiving. And then I opened my eyes, and I could still see him clearly, standing outside the window! It was then I was struck by the impossibility of it and thought, "How is it possible that Papa is stand-ing outside the car when I know he is sitting in the front seat?" Better yet, how can he continue to stand there with the car moving so fast? As this thought occurred to me, the whole picture suddenly disap-peared. I turned to look, and sure enough Marshall was still sleeping in the front seat. My left brain had kicked in and questioned the pos-sibility of this happening. And because of that, the experience ended abruptly. The mind can be a significant impediment to spiritual vision, and tends to ruin good experiences because it questions them.

I woke Patricia to tell her about this powerful and unbelievable event. It was so incredibly beautiful, and as I shared it in my low husky voice, we both became very emotional. Tears were streaming down our faces, mostly tears of gratitude. We were about to wake Marshall to tell him, but at that moment, the driver stopped the car because he was lost. I had to get out of the car to help with the direc-tions. Meanwhile, Marshall woke up, turned around and said to Patricia, "You will never believe what just happened, the incredible experience I just had." With tears now rolling down her cheeks, Patricia sat forward eagerly and said, "Oh yes, I would. Tell me!"

Marshall said that while sleeping, he felt waves of love coursing through him. Mauricio had come to him and thanked him for being a channel. Mauricio used Marshall's body as a gateway to help me. When he was alive, Mauricio never liked the idea of allowing another entity to use his body as a channel. But at that moment, he understood its healing purpose. Mauricio told Marshall to do an energization on me when we returned to Brasilia, and gave him detailed instructions on exactly what to do and what to say. We were blown away. I could hardly wait to return at the Foundation, knowing that Mauricio was going to come through Marshall and give me an energization.

When we finally arrived at Thomas's, his house was full of people. Some were waiting for healings and some were there just to be close to him. I could see that Thomas was taking his healing gifts more seriously than he had before. I also knew that from now on Mauricio would be helping his good friend from the other side. It was wonderful to see Thomas, and to share my story with him. He is so full of energy and vitality with his "RA." While his compassion for me was great, I realized the moment we arrived how unnecessary it was to have come. I guess I had thought that seeing Thomas would help me communicate with Mauricio. In actuality, my experience in the taxi with my papa and Mauricio had helped me far more.

After a short visit, we left Thomas and flew back to Brasília. Just as we were about to land, I clearly felt Mauricio's presence come onto the plane. Mauricio had always loved the moment that our plane landed in Brasília and we were home. Marshall and Patricia felt him too, so intensely in fact, that my Papa was worried about the structural integrity of the airplane. Mauricio's presence was so strong that Marshall didn't think the plane was going to be able to handle all the energy and would crash. I wasn't worried though. I knew how happy Mauricio was for us to be back in Brasilia. I remembered how much it meant to him when we would land in Brasilia together. These were always special moments.

Later, as we stood outside the airport waiting for a taxi, we could still sense Mauricio's strong presence. It stayed with us all the way back to the Foundation. Soon after we arrived, Marshall gave me the energization, praying in the way that Mauricio had told him, and calling his name aloud to invoke his energy. For me, the energization was very intimate and personal. I could only sense Mauricio. It was Mauricio's voice coming out of Marshall's body and Mauricio's touch coming out of Marshall's hands. Truly it was Mauricio. Marshall wasn't present, only his body was. I went to sleep that night with my love as close to me as he could have been if he was there physically. None of us will ever forget that night.

The next day, I left the house to turn on the generator. As I walked over to it, a great feeling of depression came over me. I felt a burden weighing me down and I wanted to flee. I didn't understand my feelings, and Patricia and Marshall were feeling the same heaviness too. We all felt that it was Mauricio, but what we didn't realize is that it was Mauricio urging us to leave.

A few days later, the boys arrived, very excited about their first plane trip alone! Seeing those angelic little bodies bounce off that plane was overwhelming. I started to cry, believing it was only because I was so happy to see them. And I was, but I was also feeling the reality that the three of us were now alone. We may be facing difficult times, but at least we were together. Marshall and Patrick were still confused about Mauricio's transition. They didn't understand how their Papa who was so strong, yet so like a child himself, could leave so suddenly. All they knew was that the last words he said to them were, "I love you my children. I come back fast, more fast than possible." It took them some time to understand that he wasn't coming back.

For the next three weeks Patricia and Marshall were my rocks, my source of strength and inspiration. They helped me face all of the difficulties involved with staying in Brasília. They knew I wasn't going anywhere. Everyone else, friends and family alike, thought that I should go back to Georgia. But my Mom and Papa didn't even try to talk me out of it. They understood my need to carry on with Mauricio's and my dream. They had a great respect for that, and they admired my courage. Their love was unconditional, and to them it didn't matter if I was right or wrong for staying. They knew I had to follow my heart.

Maybe I should have gone home and given myself time to heal. But what was truly motivating me to stay, irrational or not, was my sense of dedication. After all, this dream was as much mine as Mauricio's. It seemed like such a waste to just stop and quit now just because I was alone. Perhaps in the back of my mind I thought that being in Brasil meant I would be closer to Mauricio, even though my heart knew that he would be with me wherever I went. But I was determined to stay. I had always told Mauricio that I would continue our work in Brasil. And whenever I did, Mauricio would laugh, saying, "Kimberly, my love, if I am died, you sell all and leave Brasil very fast. This is not a country for you and the children to be alone. You will have hard times. People will take advantage of your good heart." I never really paid much attention to that, and I never thought it was ridiculous for the children and I to be there alone. I felt that nothing could stop me, that I had been put here for a reason. We hadn't worked so hard to build the Foundation, only for me to bail out in the end. I had grown to love Brasil and I was staying!

Little did I know about the tremendous obstacles in place that would try to keep me from continuing our work at the Foundation. In a meeting with Ronaldo, my lawyer, and Ruth, my friend and banker, I learned that there were complications with the title to the land. But, how was that possible? I had a house there and two other buildings under construction. As they explained the technicalities involved with the land, I knew that Mauricio had foreseen these problems, and I believed that was why his presence felt so heavy the Sunday after he died. Mauricio had known what I might innocently walk into, and he felt totally responsible. It was ironic that on the day of Mauricio's heart attack we had already scheduled a meeting with Ronaldo to transfer all of our assets into my name. Had we been able to make that meeting, these issues would have been resolved, and we wouldn't have to face the problems we were having now.

There were other problems as well. The Brasilian government was trying to throw us out of the country because I hadn't been vested with the rights of citizenship, which requires five years of residency. And although Mauricio had been in the process of legally adopting Marshall and Patrick, the boys were not yet Brasilians because the adoption papers hadn't come through before his death. So, the government thought it was necessary to deport us, and gave us 30 days to leave the country.

The obstacles appeared insurmountable, and things seemed hopeless at times. One day, soon after my meeting with Ruth and Ronaldo, I received help. As I drove the boys to our hotel in Luziania, I was suddenly inspired and very eager to get there, but it wasn't anything I could put my finger on. When we arrived, Mauricio's address book was sitting out in my room. I picked it up and it opened at the phone number of Dr. Assu, the Chefe de Gabinette, who worked directly for the President of Brasil. Without a second thought, I picked up the phone and called Dr. Assu.

Mauricio was a good friend of Dr. Assu and his wife. We had visited their home several times, and Mauricio respected him highly. On one occasion Dr. Assu had not been feeling well and I participated in his healing. This is what gave me the courage to make the call. I picked up the phone immediately and I spoke to his wife, Doña Cerene, and explained as well as I could in my limited Portuguese that I needed to see Dr. Assu. I promised that I would only take five minutes of his time. Would he be willing to listen? Doña Cerene told me to visit Dr. Assu's office at the Supreme Justice Court the next day. So off I went the following afternoon with Ronaldo, who was astounded at my success at even getting an appointment.

What I promised Doña Cerene would be a five-minute meeting, turned into two hours. I told Dr. Assu everything that had happened, focusing on our pressing immigration issues. I was mortified by how easily the government could make us leave, and the fact that they even wanted to, considering the work we had done at the Foundation and all that we gave to this growing city. I didn't want anything from this country. I only wanted to help the people. Dr. Assu loved Mauricio and greatly approved of and supported our work in Brasil. After hearing my story, he called in three colleagues, who were government ministers. They, too, were moved and the result was that, right then and there, I received documents verifying my status as a Brasilian citizen. I could not be deported. We left elated, our first victory! Ronaldo and I did a hop, skip, and a jump. I was certain this was an omen to stay. I was also sure that the whole thing had been orchestrated by Mauricio. It was too good to be true, the first positive news that I had since his death. I was very grateful and thanked Mauricio over and over for bringing his presence into that meeting.

Having overcome this major hurdle, I was sure that I could overcome the rest. With the help of Ronaldo and Mauricio's friends, I found myself able to create a new beginning. His friends knew how much Mauricio loved me, and how his life had changed when we met. They knew how unstable he had been in the past, and they recognized that Mauricio had been happier with me than he had ever been in his life. They gave me their undivided loyalty and attention. Some of them, Ronaldo in particular, insisted that I move to the city because they didn't like the idea of Marshall, Patrick and I living alone in the jungle. It could prove dangerous. After some argument I relented. It began to make sense. The boys had to go to school anyway, and there were no schools in the jungle, at least not yet.

After three weeks the moment none of us had looked forward to was upon us. Marshall and Patricia finally had to leave. They had been my source of inspiration throughout those three weeks, and as we stood on the deck of the airport in Brasília watching them board the plane, I thought I would break down and cry any moment. I didn't. Instead, I began to feel an incredible strength, a sense of well-being and love, which flowed out from me to them. The moment I dreaded had arrived, and yet I was handling it well. I wasn't alone. Mauricio was there and he was standing with me.

11

The best thing about the future is that it comes
only one day at a time.

—Abraham Lincoln

A WEEK OR SO later, my stepmother Janice arrived. She and
my Father couldn't stand the thought of the three of us alone
in Brasil, so she flew down to be with us. I don't think she
knew what she was getting herself into. There were still so many problems to solve. Not only was I dealing with issues of citizenship and residency for Marshall and Patrick, but also with legal issues involving the
Foundation and claims on Mauricio's estate by his relatives. The pressure was welling up inside of me. As difficult as it was, I also knew I
had to leave the foundation and move to the city. Marshall and Patrick
needed to be in school, and if I were going to resolve anything, I'd
have to be closer to civilization. Janice was a trooper and helped me
immeasurably. Anyone else could have folded, but not her.

The first thing we did after she arrived was to look for a new piece
of land to move the Foundation. It was a hot and dusty search.
Driving on the rough, rutted roads to these out of the way places,
you wind up swallowing tons of red-orange dust. Then we had to
walk, and I mean walk, one piece of land after another. We looked
and we looked, often walking as much as ten miles per day.
Sometimes the two of us would just stop dead in our tracks and laugh
uncontrollably, just out of sheer exhaustion. And as much as we
looked, we found nothing that even remotely compared to the foundation land. It was discouraging, and at times, it felt hopeless.

We drove all over Brasília looking for a house too. That search
took the prize. So many of the houses we visited looked like concrete

boxes, boxes which had few rooms inside. Although they had windows, there were bars over them to discourage intruders. It's like that everywhere in Brasil. I will never forget walking into one particular place and seeing cow dung everywhere. We had seen enough of that from all the hiking we had done looking for land. We also looked at an apartment building under construction. We picked our way through the construction equipment, boards, cement and whatever else was there. Nothing in the building was finished, but the owner did assure us that he would rush to have it finished. I looked around one more time. I stared at the unfinished elevator shaft and immediately I had a mental picture of Marshall and Patrick falling in it. Then I saw myself surrounded by construction workers and noises all day long. It wasn't looking good. I was used to the jungle and the natural surroundings there. On that note, we left quickly and continued our search.

Janice was wonderful, and gave of herself completely. I was very grateful to have her with me helping me put my life back together. But our time together went by much too quickly, and soon it was time for her to go. But by the time she left, I had found a simple home in Lago Sul, a nice area in Brasília, and the children were attending a private school only five miles away. There was still so much to do, but with Janice's help and support, we had made a good beginning.

The children were adjusting to their new life. They had watched Mauricio and me spend those last years constructing our lives, and then saw it all change so suddenly. It was an emotional time, but they took the changes in stride. After two months in school, they were speaking Portuguese perfectly. All of their classes were in Portuguese, except for an English class. I, on the other hand, was still struggling with my Portuguese. I decided to take lessons so that I could speak fluently. I didn't mind making mistakes, and I truly loved the language. It is rich and full of passion. I loved the way it felt when I spoke it. Sometimes, the Brasilians would laugh at my accent and I would say, "Okay, now you speak English!" They never would, even if they could, and I proved my point. But normally I would ask them to write the word I had mispronounced and teach me how to say it correctly. Day by day I found my way and learned to speak the language fairly well.

One day, about three months after Mauricio had gone, I picked the boys up from school and was driving home when Patrick, sitting in front, looked over at me and said confidently in Portuguese, "Mommy, Mommy, I just saw Papa. He is sitting down and he is eating rice and beans, and he is okay." I just looked at him, tears rolling down my cheeks. I knew when he said it to me that what he saw was true. I certainly knew how much Mauricio had loved his rice and beans, and I also knew that Patrick and Mauricio had a unique bond. I sometimes wonder if their special connection had anything to do with the day Patrick was hit by a car.

That day Mauricio, Patrick and I had lunch together in McCaysville. When we walked out of the restaurant, Patrick, who was holding Mauricio's hand, was in a playful mood. He let go of Mauricio's hand and raced ahead of us to the stoplight at the intersection. He thought he could beat the light and cross the street before we could. Mauricio saw what was going to happen the moment Patrick's hand slipped from his, but could only yell frantically for Patrick to stop. The car hit Patrick and he went down. In that moment of terror, I saw his life go before me. By the time we reached him, Patrick was back up, flitting about in shock. His head appeared to be split open and the right side of his face was cut and bruised where it had hit the ground. Blood was oozing out of his mouth.

It wasn't the driver's fault and she was beside herself with emotion. With no time to spare, we jumped into her car and rushed Patrick to the hospital. When we arrived, the doctors tried to make Mauricio and I wait in another room, but that was totally unrealistic. I wasn't about to abandon Patrick. They had to sew up his head and as they were putting in the stitches I held him with the softest embrace I knew, calming him, speaking words of love over and over. Mauricio was on the other side of Patrick, sending him healing energy. I'm sure the doctors and nurses thought we were more than a little strange. After they stitched his head and face, they had to give him a tetanus shot. Patrick had never had a shot in his life, and that was the worst part of it all for him. Twice, he ripped the needle out of his arm and away from the doctor. I thought I would die. I couldn't believe the strength of this little boy. Patrick was very stubborn.

Mauricio stayed with Patrick all night, bringing in love and energy for him, taking his pain when it became too much, and helping him to sleep. The next morning Patrick's energy was perfect, almost as if nothing had happened. He remembered only vaguely the accident and how traumatic it had been. But from that day forward, Patrick always took my hand or his Papa's when crossing a street, and never crossed without us. He was so attentive after that. His lesson was hard, but from that moment on, he always paid attention to traffic.

Patrick's words had sparked a torrent of memories and I sat outside in the car long after we arrived home. How I missed Mauricio! I remembered a night at the very beginning of our relationship when we were in London visiting friends. Mauricio and I were resting before dinner, and I asked him to meditate with me. He laughed. He had never meditated with anyone before, but he humored me and agreed to do so. We held hands and imagined a great white column of light coming down from the heavens to lift us softly, gently into the cosmos. As we lifted, I felt like I was a star dancing with another star. Then the universe became very still. It was dark, but crystal clear and it all seemed so vast. The most intense magnetic feeling of love then pulled me to my right, drawing me to a scene in which I saw Mauricio and me. He looked pretty much the same, but younger and with a slight beard. I looked the same too, only my hair was longer. As I watched, Mauricio pointed to different planets in the universe and I saw that he was teaching me about their history and the differences between them. With him I viewed these planets with great admiration and love.

I was completely immersed in the vision. I was feeling our present love within my own heart, and at the same time I felt the love of the couple I had just witnessed. When I finally opened my eyes, I had the sensation that I was still in their energy, yet back in the room. I asked Mauricio what he had just experienced. I knew that he was feeling the same thing that I was, and I wanted to know what he had seen. But he wouldn't tell me. He never did talk about it. He just grabbed me and held me, "All in good time my Kimberly, all in good time."

I finally got out of the car and went into the house. I missed Mauricio desperately, but was taking life day by day, through all the stages of my own healing. Christmas was coming, my first Christmas alone in a very long time. At least I thought I was going to be alone. But Patricia and Marshall couldn't bear the idea of my spending Christmas alone in Brasil, so they decided to come to visit us. It was a wonderful time. I got to share my sorrows, my little triumphs, and all the events taking place in our lives. We traded stories about Mauricio and our love for him. It was a quiet, special Christmas, just the children, Patricia and Marshall, and me. I would never forget this

Christmas. We had so few possessions at this time, but it didn't matter. Our hearts were full and we had gotten used to giving our things to those less advantaged. When Patricia and Marshall arrived, they bought the most outstanding ten-speed bicycles for the boys. Even though it was their only Christmas present, in their eyes it was the best and most wonderful present in the world. They only rode those bicycles for six weeks.

It was at the end of January, a day I remember clearly. To make ends meet and provide for our living expenses, I had been selling some of our personal belongings and other assets of the Foundation that we no longer needed. But some of these sales had fallen through, and I didn't have enough money to carry us through the month. Apparently Marshall and Patrick heard me crying softly in the bedroom to myself, and were aware of the problem. They'd had a meeting, and then came to me with their proposition. They decided that if each of them sold their bicycles, then we would have enough money for the coming month. I remember looking up at them through my teary eyes, not believing what I had just heard. They looked so mature standing there, excited about their plan to help. I couldn't help myself. I burst out crying at this unselfish act, and even more at the purity of their love for me. God demonstrated his love that day and spoke to me through my children. There is always an answer to each of life's problems, and we are always provided for by our Heavenly Father who loves us unconditionally. I was lifted, and just like that, the problem was solved. The bicycles were in high demand, and they sold very quickly, within a day. That bought us a little more time. I delighted over my children's selflessness and how God touched me through these little ones.

In March of 1994, I scheduled some private RoHun appointments with people in Boston. I had chosen to go on the road again to earn a living. It would be my first trip back to the U.S. in a long while. The children would stay home in Brasil. How difficult it was to leave them! The boys were traumatized, especially Marshall. I'll never forget the look on his face at the airport gate. He was panic stricken as he looked into my eyes, suddenly realizing that I was about to leave. Then he became hysterical. He held onto me pleading with me not to go. There was no way I was getting on the plane with Marshall feeling that way, so I held him tightly, let him feel my presence, and just loved him. I felt his fear, understood it and assured him that I would be back "more fast than possible." I let him feel my calmness, my presence for a while, and then I had him look into my eyes. By then, Marshall had calmed down, and his breathing was almost normal. He looked at me with such trusting eyes as I told him my reason for leaving, and with each passing moment, he got stronger and stronger. I promised to call him and Patrick every evening so that they could hear my voice and know that I was okay. We kissed goodbye and off I went.

My trip began with a few days in Georgia to visit my family. I wasn't ready to stay in the home that Mauricio and I had built there, so I stayed with Patricia and Marshall. That night, Patricia, Marshall and I watched the movie Sleepless In Seattle. In the first few minutes, the film shows the lead character at his wife's grave. He was completely and madly in love with her, and she had just died. He was lost and full of grief. As I watched, my own emotions rose to the surface and tears of sadness quietly streamed down my face. Suddenly Patricia turned off the movie saying, "Mauricio's here, let's meditate."

We joined hands, and the communication began almost instantly. I was emotional and unable to see clearly, but I could feel my feelings stirring in his incredible presence. Almost immediately, Mauricio began to speak to me through my papa, Marshall. He told me how much he loved me and that this kind of love could never die. He said that I would even love again one day, and I wasn't to feel it as a betrayal of him. He continued, telling me that I needed to move on with my life and my purpose, and that he wanted me to be happy. He told me that we had work to do, but that now, I should rest my mind. I could feel him lift burdens from my heart as he told me that everything was okay.

I didn't think for one minute that I would ever fall in love again, so that part about finding love again didn't faze me. But in everything else, it was as if Mauricio knew my thoughts and knew all about the difficulties I was having in Brasil. I began to understand that he was worried about me being there. He gave me numerous reasons why I should be home in the U.S. instead of in Brasil, and he felt very strongly that I belonged at Delphi.

I wasn't ready to accept that yet. But because of this experience, the following day I mustered up the courage to go home, accompanied by my Mom. It was very curious. Although the house was empty and everything had been put in storage, it didn't feel that way at all. Sometimes homes feel abandoned when you leave them, but our house was alive and well, and it had an energy all of its own. The air inside felt crisp and clean and we could feel its vibrant energy. Feeling that energy, a calm and peacefulness came over me. It was the first peace I had felt in a while. I knew I was still very much in my healing process, but I never thought my life would feel like such a roller coaster. I didn't know where I was headed, except that I was going to Boston to do RoHun, and then back to Brasília to my children. But I knew that I was okay and very much protected, and that my destiny lay in the hands of God.

RoHun is an energy-based therapy that works to clear blockages in the chakras, the energy centers of the body. I loved helping others clear their energy blocks and heal through RoHun. During this Boston trip, I did four and five sessions a day that lasted up to two hours each. Each day I was drained emotionally, and the work took its toll on me physically. I was in bed by 8:30 every night out of sheer exhaustion.

On March 15, the eve of Mauricio's birthday, I was determined to stay awake until midnight so that I could light a candle for him. I was always big on birthdays and on this particular one, I had a strong need to feel close to him. I didn't know why I was making such a big deal out of it, other than it was the first time on his birthday that we weren't together. I wished with all my heart that I could be with him and I spoke my desire aloud. I managed to stay awake, and at midnight I lit a candle, said a prayer, and lay down to meditate myself to sleep. The next thing I knew, I was walking down a beautiful winding path. There was another path adjacent to this one, and ahead, the two paths became one. There were flowers and bushes everywhere, and my senses were alive with all the different smells. There was a feeling of celebration in the air. I was wearing a white dress and holding two flowers in my hand. I felt beautiful.

I continued walking on the path to the pool where a party was going on. I didn't know who or what the party was for, but I was drawn to the pool. I sat down beside it and began to stare into the water. There were people everywhere, mostly members of my family. As I glanced up to see what was going on, Mauricio appeared before me. I gasped. I was so surprised that I stood up quickly and touched him saying, "Mauricio, you're really here. You came!" I was so amazed, I couldn't take my eyes off of him. His physical presence was exactly as I knew it, except that now his body looked fresh and free. His hair was just as white, if not more so, and it was flowing. And the pain that he seemed to carry in life was now gone too. He was just too good to be true. He looked so real that I had to look again to see if he was. So I reached out to touch him to make sure. He took his hand and moved it over his throat, telepathically telling me that he was unable to speak as of yet. He was still adjusting to this dimension. Somehow I understood him perfectly, and I waited.

We searched deeply into each other's eyes. I could tell by his look that he knew everything about me. My heart was beating rapidly. I wanted to know everything that he had been doing since he had left. I knew so little about that. My sister, Kelly, walked over and asked me whom I was talking to. I was surprised that she had even asked, and I said to her excitedly, "I'm talking to Mauricio. Don't you see him?" She replied, "No, I don't," and her eyes filled with tears. Her emotions were strong. I was anxious for Kelly to see Mauricio, and I told her without hesitation to squeeze her eyes shut tightly three times and then to open them again, and she would see him. She did, and when she opened her eyes she could see him and she began to cry tears of joy. When Mauricio touched Kelly on the forehead, she could only look at him. She had no words, but their eyes spoke of an understanding between them. Then he looked at me and said, "It's time my love, time to go. It is time to rest."

In the blink of an eye we were in a lovely hotel room like the ones we stayed in when we traveled. I was in the bathroom and we were getting ready for bed. To me it felt exactly like before he left. I still wanted to talk, to know everything that he was doing. I could clearly see that Mauricio was a much higher being of light. He told me he was working in the higher spiritual dimensions, as well as in the astral planes, with research teams of a highly enlightened consciousness. He was studying and investigating the nature of the universe, and the many realms of light. He was working with many other light beings who he was assigned to work with and help the many dedicated people here on earth.

Mauricio told me about political events taking shape, and that there would be much turbulence associated with them. He talked about problems related to the Presidency of the United States. He told me that a scandal would occur, and that the country would come to a crossroads that had the potential to shift our collective consciousness and force us to choose the way in which we would relate to our world in the future. He said it was the very beginning, the beginning of the end, and the ending of our lives in the world as we know it. He told me there would be great changes to come, and that we as a people would never be the same. I listened intently, not fully realizing the depth of his message in our conversation. He then reminded me of all of those times that he corrected me about the concept of time. "Don't ever think that time is time. Time is not time as we know it," he said. "Time is an energy, and you will never understand time until you understand it as an energy." What he was saying is that we think of time as hard and fast, moving endlessly second by second, minute by minute, and hour after hour. But energy doesn't act in this way. Energy forms and moves and is always changing. As a spiritual being you don't live by time, you live by sequence. You could say a sequence is time, but it is not time because a sequence is not over until you fulfill the sequence. As soon as you fulfill the sequence for spiritual learning then you go on to the next sequence. One sequence may be a year and the next sequence may be three months. So, your life progression down the Seven-Day Journey, the journey of creation, is a series of progressive sequences. And you are the one in control of how long or short those sequences last, because in the highest sense, you are in control. You are the one who is evolving, and you are the one who is making the choices, good or bad. Arthur Ford often said, "If you can change one thought of a person in one life time you have done a miracle." In this state of awareness it all felt so impressive and so simple. I knew this knowledge was cosmic, for he had reiterated this message so many times before. But only now I understood.

Then Mauricio took a long look at me. With pure love emanating from those honeysuckle-brown eyes he said, "It's time, my love. We have work to do. But now, you must rest with me." I lay down in the bed with his arms around me and melted into his love. I was home. I was safe. I was loved.

When I opened my eyes, I was back in Peter's guest room looking at the candle. It was 4:00 a.m. and I couldn't believe what had just happened! I had been gone for four hours. I was blown away by my dream, and energized beyond belief. My gratitude overflowed and I cried for the joy that I was feeling. What a gift I was given! It was Mauricio's birthday but I had received one of the most special presents of all. I lay awake the rest of the night contemplating this experience. I thought that I would pay for my sleeplessness but, in the morning, I knew I could easily get through the day. I was inspired! I had more energy than I can remember having in a long time. My heart was radiating so much warmth, and because of that, I was able to do some of my best work. I shared that energy with all of the clients who came to see me on that special day, March 16, 1994.

When I returned to Brasil, I had time to think and evaluate everything that had happened to me, and what my future was to be or not to be. I was feeling as though events were conspiring to push me out of Brasil, and after going to Delphi, I had the nagging thought that it might be time to let go and come home. But I felt real resistance to leaving, and I rationalized once again my need to stay. The children were finally settled. They loved their school and had very nice friends. The three of us were building a life together here, so I stubbornly continued to pursue Mauricio's and my dream, until that Saturday morning in May in the middle of a thunderstorm. I was on my way home from the grocery store with my nanny, Sonya, and her four year-old son, João. Without warning, the car began to hydroplane as we approached the bridge over the Lago Paranoa. The river was very deep here. I was afraid we would hit the car on our right, so I cut the wheel to the left. The car swerved violently and I lost control. It felt like we were moving in slow motion as the car veered across the oncoming lanes and went over the side of a little embankment just before hitting the first strut of the bridge.

When we landed at the bottom of the hill, we were only a foot from the drop off to the water. Sonya and I looked at each other in shock. We were badly shaken, but bruised knees were the only injury we had to show from this mishap. Sonya's son was sobbing with fright, but he was also fine. I couldn't believe it. By all rights, we should have been dead. It was then that cold reality crept in. I realized that this accident was no accident. It was a sign, a sign to which I should pay attention.

My work in Brasil was not proceeding smoothly, and it appeared that people and events were conspiring to keep me from fulfilling our dream. Just as quickly as one door would open, another would slam shut, and I had to start over again and again. Was I tempting fate by staying in Brasil? How far was I willing to go? Did I want to die? Was my purpose somewhere else and not here? At that point, I realized that I should listen more carefully to my heart and not my desires. I realized that it was my purpose to live, and to live life fully. I didn't want to test the hands of fate, and I no longer felt like resisting my destiny. I began to accept what I felt in my heart, and for the first time I accepted that it was time to go home. I was meant to fulfill my work in another way. Maybe the sequence of my life here was finished, and this is what Mauricio was saying when he reminded me about the concept of time.

12

The Lord is my shepherd,
I shall not want.

—Psalm 23

THE APPLAUSE OF the passengers as we landed startled me and brought me back to reality. The flight from Sao Paolo to Miami was timeless. I had been in a world all of my own. It was hard to believe that we had finally arrived. The thought of going through customs with 13 bags and my children in tow wasn't something, which I was looking forward to. But I was sure when they took one look at us they would waive us through. We hadn't even gotten off the plane yet and I was feeling the burden. I hadn't slept the entire flight, and already I was exhausted. After the long journey from Brasil, going from Miami to Atlanta seemed easy. We all spoke Portuguese because Patrick was unable to speak English, and even though I was an American, I felt like a foreigner.

I'll never forget stepping out of the airport and seeing the big motor home waiting for us and all of our worldly possessions, packed in those 13 bags. Touché, I thought, as I smiled to myself. When Mauricio first came to Delphi, he too was picked up in our big motor home. I can remember thinking how absurd it was to drive a vehicle like this to the airport to pick up one or two people. Back then I wondered, "Who is this man? What is he, special?" And, now here I was being picked up in the same manner, although admittedly, we had a lot more to carry.

With all the hard knocks I had taken in Brasil, I could have felt bitter. I could have felt that I was the poor unwitting victim of circumstance. But I made a different choice. I knew that all of my spiritual training had prepared me for exactly this kind of situation, and I had to rise to the occasion or test. I was discouraged and disheartened about leaving, but this was only a temporary setback. In life we can't be setback unless we are moving forward. In the end, my heart chose love. I wanted to learn about love and all that it means. I wanted to understand and know myself through this love, and know that with love I could overcome any obstacle. I know that I am love and it's my love that has the power to conquer all the tests and challenges that come before me. If I learned anything from Mauricio, it was this. And if I had lived a loving life with him, how could I ever settle for anything less than that again? Had I chosen to sink, to despair, then all of the spiritual understanding I gained through my experience with Mauricio and in my life would have been in vain. I was not a victim. I had chosen the events and circumstances of my life in order to grow spiritually and evolve. My heart still belonged to me. I chose love and that felt good. My purpose in life was to bring spirit into matter, a simple task, nothing grandiose. That is all I ever wanted to do.

It felt right to be going back to the Blue Ridge Mountains, back to Georgia, but I was also anxious and uncertain. I didn't know exactly what I would be doing, but I had many options at the Delphi School, and I loved the work I had always done there. But I also knew I couldn't work in quite the same way now. I wasn't the same person and I needed to stretch myself again spiritually. I wanted something new to inspire me to reach greater heights. I wanted to give and be received in new and wondrous ways.

When we arrived home, Marshall and Patrick raced off to see everybody, and I was alone. The house that Mauricio and I had shared felt empty to me now, and my heart began to feel empty too. I walked into the living room and opened one of the packing crates that were randomly strewn around the house. Just inside was a picture of Mauricio and me on the cover of the magazine *Psychology Today*. It was one of those simulated magazine covers available at amusement parks and similar places. Mauricio looked so animated and beautiful in that picture that waves of longing flowed through me. The indescribable loss of my best friend, my husband, this wonderful expression of God's Light, prompted me to speak aloud to him. I spoke to the air, telling Mauricio how much I loved him and how much we missed him. I asked him quite loudly, if he was happy now that I was home. I was emotional. Tears were streaming down my face.

When I looked down at the picture, tears were also flowing from Mauricio's eyes. I blinked, sure that my own tears were blurring my vision. But when I put my finger out to touch Mauricio's tears, I drew them away wet. Then I smelled the sweetest aroma in the room, and a sense of deep, profound peace came over me. It was then I knew that unlike my own, Mauricio's tears were tears of joy. Now that I was at home, he was at peace, and I sensed that he would be even closer now, and that somehow we would be working together in a new way. It was all still a mystery to me.

We spent the next six months adapting to yet another new life. As I had feared on the plane, Patrick had a very difficult time because he couldn't remember his native language. The other children laughed at his pronunciation and his accent. And to compound the problem, the school system insisted on holding Patrick back a grade. Despite Patrick's difficulties, he remained sweet and open to his new experiences. Sometimes he expressed a maturity that was way beyond his years. I was always learning something from him. Often when he knew I was feeling discouraged with our little town, he would often say, "Mommy, maybe we have to bring the purpose here and spread the light in order to help change the people, or maybe nobody else would."

Marshall had an easier time adjusting to life in the States. He remembered much more English than Patrick and, as the more gregarious of the two, had less trouble handling the culture of the North Georgia hills. But Marshall had other problems. I began working again and traveling a lot, and whenever I left fear haunted him. At first, I thought this was very strange because we had always traveled a lot, especially Marshall, who had flown everywhere with me since he was a baby. Since they were very young, both boys had flown often between the U.S., Brasil, and other parts of the country, and were accustomed to seeing me leave. It had never been an issue before. But now, before each and every trip, I had to sit with Marshall, comforting him and promising over and over again, that no harm would come to me and I would return safe and sound.

Then one day as I looked into my son's eyes, a light came on. I realized why he felt this way. He had never gotten the opportunity to say good-bye to his Papa. Mauricio had promised him that he would come back soon, but he never did. Marshall's overwhelming fear was that if I left, he could lose me too. I couldn't believe how blind I had been. What was I thinking? I know energy, and I know that energy sometimes gets stuck. I also know that when upsetting events take place, they can trigger deep insecurities. Through healing, these kinds of feelings can be transmuted and the thoughts that are connected to the feelings can be transformed. I chided myself for not doing something sooner. I called my Mom and asked her to do an emergency RoHun session with Marshall. Although I had done RoHun on both boys many times, this was clearly a job for Patricia's clarity and objectivity.

My mother founded the RoHun processes in 1983. RoHun therapy blends spiritual and psychological processes together in a unique way. It reaches deep down into a person's subconscious to discover the energy blocks that produce self-limitation or negative feelings of self. The person discovers the negative thought or behavior pattern that is causing the block, and through a process of understanding and forgiveness, the block is cleared, and healing occurs. RoHun gives profound insight into inner problems very quickly, because the client is able to see themselves from a spiritual perspective and not just a physical one. It is truly a modern miracle given to us by Spirit to allow us to grow and evolve quickly and effectively.

Marshall's therapy sessions revealed his fear to him by taking him back into his memories. Once he was in the energy, she then had him separate from the emotion of it so he could look at it objectively and see clearly how it was affecting his life. Through this understanding, Marshall's loving self, his spiritual side, could see that the fear was only a part of him, not all of him, and he could consciously reduce its hold over him. In two sessions, Marshall healed his fear and, having released it, was able to talk to Mauricio and say goodbye. He was able to release Mauricio into the light knowing he would always be near by when he needed him. Marshall made his peace and when he did, the healing took place instantly. Marshall's fear was transformed and the difference in him was clearly noticeable. He never cried again when I had to travel, and he always said to me, "Don't worry Mommy, I know you are coming back."

Children are natural-born healers. When they are motivated by love, their energies are naturally channeled into good. Not only was Marshall's energy more positive, but he started sharing this positive attitude with others. Soon after Marshall's healing, I was doing some healing work with my friend Meg. Her daughter Cierra was very upset and crying hysterically, and would not let us out of her sight. She was apparently very sensitive to the energy in the room and kept thinking that something was going to happen to her mother. We couldn't work with Cierra there, so my friend Linda decided to take all the kids to the llama farm. But Cierra screamed so loudly and fought so hard, we couldn't even get her into the car. Marshall, who was already in the back seat, reached out his hand to call her into the car. To him she listened. He said, "Don't worry, Cierra, your Mommy isn't going anywhere. She lives right here." And then Marshall took Cierra's hand and placed it over her heart. "Anytime you want to see and feel your Mommy, you can close your eyes with your hands on your heart, and your Mama will be there. You can see her too."

Cierra listened intently to Marshall, and she calmed down and went to the llama farm without protest. The next day, Meg called to tell me about the effect Marshall had on Cierra. That morning, as she did everyday, Meg started to get out of the car to walk her daughter into school. But Cierra stopped her before she got out and said, "It's okay Mommy, I can walk in by myself." She put one hand on her mother's heart and the other on her own heart, and said, "I know you are with me. You live here and I can see you whenever I want."

The first six months back in the US was a whirlwind of continuous events that were establishing our new life together. On one occasion the friend of a woman who was dying of cancer contacted me. Her friend had heard about Mauricio and other Brasilian healers, and she called to ask if I would help arrange a trip to Brasil and act as their guide. The dying woman was a medical doctor who didn't believe in anything spiritual, much less spiritual healing. She didn't even understand the concept, but she had heard of the incredible healings that sometimes happen in Brasil, and had decided to turn to these healers for help. She was desperate for something to save her life, and was convinced that she would find that something in Brasil

I was resistant to the idea. It seemed like a very long trip for someone who was so desperately ill, had no connection to Spirit, and did not recognize the spiritual qualities of her own soul. I thought, "My God, this woman is a MD. She would die right here and now at the notion that one of these healers wanted to do surgery on her with a kitchen knife or poke around inside her body with large needles!" I tried to talk her out of going altogether, suggesting healing alternatives in this country that I thought could be beneficial to her. But no matter what I suggested, she refused. She had her mind made up that nothing else would do and she was going to Brasil with or without me. I could feel her desperation, and my misgivings melted into compassion. I took a chance and made the calls to Brasil, knowing that it still wasn't certain because trips such as this one required a great deal of preparation and in some cases luck. But the timing was perfect. Everything flowed smoothly, and the arrangements were easily made. I naively took that as a positive sign. So off we went in their private jet, the woman, her husband, her brother and the friend.

I was excited to be returning to Brasil, but I was also apprehensive about this trip. I knew very little about these people except that the woman and her husband were well established in the medical field, and her family owned a large winery. I soon discovered how much they all lacked in spiritual understanding. They were upscale, linear people who were grasping at one last straw to save this woman's life. The woman's friend was the most open and receptive of the group, and it was clear that she was providing their emotional strength and support.

We had a stopover deep in the Amazon jungle, where we spent the night. After dinner, I prepared them for what was to come.

I told them that this experience would be very different than what they were accustomed to in the United States where everything is clean and sterile. I also tried to tell them about the phenomena that often accompanied the healings. Phenomena are a daily occurrence in Brasil, and "healing phenomena" are well documented among Brasilians, although there is no scientific or medical explanation for them. This was a subject foreign to all of them, but the family friend. They weren't even sure they believed in phenomena, for the unknown had been a subject that had never really come up in their lives until now.

Later that evening, I did some healing work on the woman with the intention of helping to lift her energies into a greater state of awareness and sensitivity, so that she could better receive the healing from Dr. Guedes. Her body responded very well. She became stronger and more open and relaxed, and was able to make the rest of the trip without pain. But I was still worried. I knew we were in trouble when she said that her faith in me was growing, but that she had little faith in God, and that it was hard for her to trust or rely on a God who could do this to her. I felt the futility in her voice as she spoke. If she believed that there was no greater source, no God, then from where would her salvation come? Where was the hope for her healing if she couldn't connect with anything greater than the physical world? I couldn't seem to make her understand that. I couldn't just pour the truth into her-she had to feel it. In fact, I couldn't do anything to influence her on my own.

From working with Mauricio, I learned clearly that true healing always takes place through God's will, not self-will. People have specific lessons to learn in life, and sometimes those lessons are learned through physical illness. Our physical illnesses signal a time for us to grow spiritually. The physical body is the receiver of all subtle influences. Over time, faulty thoughts and repressed negative emotions will ultimately manifest in the physical body as Dis-ease (the absence of ease) or some other physical problem. Disease then becomes a friend, a teacher that helps us to grow and learn what we have not learned or could not learn in any other way. It creates the opportunity to turn inward, to discover the thoughts and feelings that have created the disease. And it gives us the chance to heal with the energies of understanding, love and forgiveness. We are then prepared for the next step of our spiritual evolution. Sometimes this next step includes letting go of the physical and material world and accepting the transition into our next space. After trying to explain these things to the woman in a way that she could understand, I gave up. She needed to be guided very gently, as she was not quite ready to open herself to all of the possibilities available. I prayed for her and her next step, whatever that was to be.

The next day we flew to São Paulo for our appointment with Dr. Guedes. After a short wait, we entered the healing sanctuary. Over one hundred people sat on one side of the large room, silently praying while waiting for their names to be called. On the other side of the room at a large table were fifteen or twenty mediums channeling ectoplasm. We sat down and watched as Dr. Guedes put his needles deeply into one of the eyes of a patient. My group was horrified, astonished that the woman did not cry out in agony. They were medical doctors, and this kind of procedure was completely outside of their experience and beyond their understanding. They couldn't understand how something like this was possible. It didn't look safe, and because it wasn't sterile, it couldn't be safe! They immediately reacted and decided there was no way they would let Dr. Guedes work on the ill woman. I looked over at her and looked directly into her eyes and said, "We have come a long way. What do you have to lose? You have nothing to lose. I will be there for you." She looked at me, stunned. She was appalled. I could feel her anxiety and her struggle. We continued watching Dr. Guedes work on others, sticking his needles through the upper part of the people's arms and legs, in various parts of their backs or stomachs, through the head, anywhere he felt a need. Sometimes he would use a knife to augment the needles. Not once did he use an anesthesia. It was unnecessary. After a few hours, they began to get curious and began to seriously consider allowing Dr. Guedes to do the healing.

Dr. Guedes already knew their discomfort about being there. After all he was a sensitive. He kept us sitting there in the energy watching until the very end, and called us up only after he had finished with everyone else. First he worked on the friend of the family who had back problems from an old injury. You could see the relief on her face as the needles penetrated into her back without pain. She felt the energy and she could feel the difference. After the surgery she was able to sit up straight and without pain, something that she could not do before. This inspired the others to go too. The sick woman was now ready.

Dr. Guedes began working with her, but after several minutes he told me in Portuguese that he could not help her. Her sickness had progressed too far, and had already taken a great toll upon her. He said that what would help the most would be for her to make peace with her life and begin to heal the anger that was so prominent in her energy field. He worked with her as best he could, but he had spoken with finality. I was sad for her, but I understood his message. I just couldn't tell them what Dr. Guedes said. I couldn't take away their hope so soon. They needed time to prepare. Besides, the next morning we would be flying to Pose Allegre to see Thomas Green Morton, the other "light man," and there was no telling what miraculous things might occur during his healing. If nothing else I knew that these experiences were helping to open her to her next stage of development.

After we returned to the hotel there was a lot to digest, and they were having a difficult time of it. Perhaps the sick woman sensed what had happened, because soon after our return, she turned very negative and became extremely upset about her experience. I watched her turn on herself, and then I watched as the others got sucked into her fear and negativity. The truth of the matter was that they couldn't accept what they had seen. They couldn't handle the experience. They had no point of reference in their minds to explain what had just happened.

They began questioning and discounting the entire experience. They were no longer open to my counsel and the sick woman began to blame me for involving her with Dr. Guedes in the first place. She was convinced she would get AIDS because she believed that Dr. Guedes used un-sterilized needles on her, and insisted that everyone in the group now had to be tested for AIDS. She even convinced the family friend, who had had a wonderful experience, that she would be irresponsible if she didn't tell her husband about the possibility of AIDS. Her husband had known she was going to Brasil, but he hadn't known exactly why.

I was disheartened. My worst fear about the trip had come to pass. She wasn't ready. The concept of spiritual surgery was beyond her because deep down she was not receptive enough to open to anything new. Her beliefs were set, and her fear was safer for her because it was what she had always known. As we boarded the airplane, I knew going home would be the longest trip of my life. I had to breathe in courage, and breathe out my feelings of frustration. I had to hold on to what I knew to be the truth. I didn't know what to do except to let some time pass. We were leaving all so suddenly. I sat in my seat, staring out the window, praying for an answer. I was compelled to speak to the family friend, who had been the most open of the group. I went and sat down beside her. I asked her quietly to close her eyes and to remember her own experience in her heart. I told her to trust that an answer of truth would come if she would ask for confirmation. She did as I asked, and a few minutes later, the good feeling she had after leaving Dr. Guedes returned. We were both thankful and I knew that it would only be a matter of time when she would get her answer. In some strange way I felt relieved.

We landed in Curacao for the night, but I was not looking forward to our stay there. All I could think about was getting home. We met in the hotel dining room for dinner, and everyone was very subdued until the family friend bounced in happily announcing that all was well. She had just spoken to her husband but, before she was able to confess why she had gone to Brasil, he told her that an old friend, a psychic, had dropped by and said to him, "Don't tell me where your wife is. I see her surrounded by many people, and I can see long needles being used. Whatever she is experiencing, it is a good thing. I can see that she is in good hands." When she shared why she had gone to Brasil, her husband told her not to worry, that he had complete confidence in her. She knew without a shadow of a doubt that this was her confirmation, and all of her previous fears and doubts lifted.

As she shared her story, I silently thanked God. She was their rock after all. She brought ease back into the group and they let go of the idea that they had been given AIDS by the needles. For the remainder of our trip home, the group was more open-minded. As we neared the private airstrip in Marietta, Georgia, I wondered what lesson I was to take away from all of this. My inner strength had been called upon, but I was used to that. I knew that the trip hadn't been in vain, even though I also knew in my heart that the woman wouldn't be alive in another month. I really couldn't say what the lesson was, so I just accepted the experience for what it was, and trusted that divine order was at work.

I walked off that plane knowing I had done the best I could, and was comforted with this realization. I sent prayers to the woman every evening for a week, planting seeds for her enlightenment. I also spoke to her soul telepathically, nurturing her need for Spirit in this life and the life that would follow after she passed on. It was time for her to recognize that she was connected to a greater source of power, a source far greater than the human self. It was her chance to forgive and let go, and maybe even let God back into her heart. Three weeks later she died.

13

Tis love that makes me bold and resolute, Love
that can find a way where path there's none, of
all the gods the most invisible.

—Euripedes

DURING MY FIRST year back in the United States, I still
missed Mauricio desperately. But since I had been back in
Georgia, I felt even closer to him. The communication
between us had not only increased, but my vision was extremely open
and clear. During this time it helped that Mauricio did little things
around the house to let us know he was still nearby, loving and supporting us. Sometimes when the children were fighting or arguing, a
toy or other object would fly off the table and across the room. The
boys knew instantly that it was their Papa telling them to stop, and
they always did. They always ran to find me and tell me, "Papa is here."

One night, I left the boys in the care of a babysitter. When I got
home, I found the sitter very antsy, and the look on her face was one
of anxiety. She couldn't wait to get out of our house. I hadn't cooked
all day, but the aroma of rice and beans permeated the entire house.
The babysitter searched everywhere looking for the source of this
smell. She was worried because she thought something could be
burning. Finally, the boys told her not to worry, that it was only their
Papa, back from the other side cooking his dinner. Strangely enough,
this did not reassure her and she never came back to sit with Marshall
and Patrick again.

I often spoke aloud to Mauricio and sometimes as I talked, a brief
flash of light would come from the wall or ceiling, and I knew he was
letting me know that he was listening. But I was still having trouble
sleeping through the night. I was constantly going from upstairs to

downstairs, in order to find things to do that would distract me from going to sleep. I would usually end up dozing a few hours on the sofa in the living room. Often as I lay there, my mind would conjure up wonderful memories of Mauricio and I, and our time together in this very house. Our life had revolved around spirituality, and in the evenings we often meditated or read, discussing passages from the Bible. Our home was our spiritual retreat. It always felt sacred here.

Mauricio did all of the electrical work in the house. How many times I saw him check the breakers. He never knew if they were on or off, so he would stick his finger into the socket and say, "Yes, it is on." Whenever he touched the exposed 220-volt wires, my heart would always stop, waiting for something to happen. I thought that he should have been thrown across the room like any normal human being, but not Mauricio. He would always wear a big grin and say, "No problem." We were the only ones in McCaysville who could get eleven television stations with just a simple antenna on the roof, a feat that is really impossible in this town. The closest broadcast stations were 70 miles over the high mountains, or 120 miles to the south. As full of electricity and as gifted as he was working with it, Mauricio was afraid of lightning and thunderstorms. He never liked to walk in the woods when there was an electrical storm. He feared that lightning would strike him and hurt him.

Mauricio and I shared many close times with my best friend Linda. The three of us often stayed up all night talking about life and the mysteries of the universe. Mauricio worked with both Linda and me, giving us what he called Initiation, a process that took us through spiritual gateways so that we could experience higher levels of cosmic or universal understanding. During these initiations my chakras always felt like intertwined balls of energy spiraling through and around my body, and I truly felt a oneness with All That Is. I could feel my energy connected to the trees, the stars, everything that had an existence. This feeling lasted for days afterward, sometimes weeks. I didn't have a clue then that I was being prepared for future events, but I should have known.

One night, after working with a very receptive group at Delphi, Mauricio and I were getting ready to go home. Mauricio had really outdone himself and we were both feeling elevated from the experience with the group. Jokingly, I asked, "Mauricio, what will we do one day when you're not around to give energization to us all?" He turned and looked at me very deliberately and said, "Ah, Kimberly, one day it will be you who will give energization." I laughed, "Not possible, my love, that is your karma, besides I don't make light." With a humble reply Mauricio said, "Kimberly, you have psychical light. You have a gift, and your gift is love. All people need to know love. It is love that will lead them to the beautiful light that is within them, that connects them to an even bigger source of light. You need only this."

Now, months later, as I lay on the sofa in our house, Mauricio's words rang in my head over and over. I had never really thought much about that conversation again until now. We had never talked much about the time when he wouldn't be with me, even though we both knew he would pass on before I did. I hadn't wanted to think about that, and I certainly never thought that I would be the one to carry on his work. But laying there on the sofa my heart opened, and suddenly I felt a longing, a longing for energization. Only now, I wanted to do one! I felt intrigued at the very thought of it. Immediately waves of energy washed over me. I was inspired and began thinking about all of the people to whom I could give. A moment later I was besieged by doubt. I thought, "I can't do an energization. That's Mauricio's job. I don't have the lights or anything else to help me." As soon as these doubts appeared in my mind, they were swept away by an invisible force that I knew instinctively was Mauricio. I couldn't see him, but I could feel his presence. The room was buzzing with energy, and my heart was beating strongly, anticipating what was next.

I was finally beginning to understand why, during those last six months of his life, he began to work with me extremely close. He knew he would be leaving soon. We had always worked together before. But during this time, Mauricio became much more serious about sharing his knowledge and wisdom. Whenever I asked him a question about a spiritual experience I had, he never answered directly. Instead, he would make me search within myself for the answers and share with him my insight. Even though this often frustrated me, it made me stronger. I had to reach deeper and deeper and open myself even more, to discover the truth of the experience.

During our last six months together, Mauricio was strengthening our cosmic connection and helping to prepare the way for me to continue his work. As I lay there in reflection, all the little things he ever told me came flooding back. It all made perfect sense. I realized I had been his apprentice all along. I just never thought about it in that way. Then I remembered my dream in which he told me, "It's time, my love. We have work to do." I now knew what he had been talking about. With Mauricio's faith in me so strong, how could I let him down or for that matter God? I felt confident, and made the commitment at that very moment. And after I made this decision, I felt the pieces fall into place and, for the first time since I had been back in the U.S., I felt clear about my future and what I was going to do. I did my first energization on my mother, and the second on my Papa. Then I worked on whoever was willing to let me. I had found my place once more, and I was home again.

Mauricio had never really instructed me on how to do an energization. But because he worked on me so often, and I was with him day and night, I knew just what to do. At first, I was afraid to cry out "energia, forca, harmonia" and call upon the Brother Lights. But when I did, I felt the grace of God move through me. I felt the sacredness and the deep love flow through me to the person with whom I was working.

As I gave more and more energizations, I knew I could bring that sacred energy through for everyone who needed to find their way to the light and experience their connection with God. My path was confirmed when people began seeking me out for this experience. Almost as soon as I began this work, I received wonderful confirmations. Many people saw light inside their heads, some experienced the euphoric feeling of bliss that comes with a sacred or spiritual experience, and others even felt their Kundalini rising. Each time I did one, I had more and more confidence in this energy, and I was able to command it to come with even greater conviction. I continued on this path, doing as many sessions as I could.

After arriving home one evening from a trip to Ohio, during which I had done thirty energizations in three days, I was totally exhausted. I walked upstairs, and when I reached the bedroom, I felt a tightening in my chest and my left arm began to tingle, as if it was going numb. Thinking I was having a heart attack, I immediately sat down on the bed. I was trembling. My heart was racing and I thought that at any minute, I would spin out of control. I managed to pick up the phone and call my sister, Kelly, who lived close by. I knew I needed help, fast. Kelly came over quickly and helped me make my way down to the living room, where I lay in the middle of the floor. She wanted to call an ambulance, but I would have none of it. After arguing with me, she could see it was no use and that I wouldn't go. So she called my Mom. I was shaking more and more violently with each passing moment. When Patricia and Marshall arrived a short time later, my body was already experiencing uncontrollable convulsions. My blood pressure was extremely high and my heart was beating a mile a minute.

Marshall sat down on the floor next to me. He put his hand over my solar plexus chakra and started sending me energy. I went into a trance-like state and my consciousness began to lift. I saw Mauricio just as clear as day standing directly behind Marshall, looking concerned and beckoning to me with an outstretched hand. Without hesitation I took his hand, and soon we were traveling up into the universe. Then I saw a huge thick bubble, a sphere of light. We entered the sphere and we continued traveling upward. I knew that Mauricio was aware of where he was taking me. It felt so far away. It felt like I was going home.

As we continued upward, more spheres appeared and we traveled through these as well. It was all so vast. Then we became the spheres themselves. I still felt Marshall's energy and knew that his presence was there too, traveling with us, one with us on this journey. Then we stopped. As I stood in front of Mauricio he began working with my energy, smoothing and calming it. His appearance was so powerful and radiant that I was mesmerized by it. He looked at me very lovingly and said, "Oh my love, you are fragile. Don't make this. You have much to give, not necessary you give your life, too." He smiled and his energy went through me. I immediately understood. He anointed me and then gave a special blessing as he touched my forehead.

The problem was that in the session when I said, "I give part of my life for you," I actually did just that. By using those exact words, I was giving away my own personal life force, giving part of my own energy to each individual. He was telling me not to say this when doing energization. It wasn't necessary, and I needed to keep my own vitality. As soon as he was finished, Mauricio began leading me back through the spheres of light, back to the living room where Marshall still sat with his hand on my stomach. I opened my eyes and felt an incredible peace. I had been gone for an entire hour, and during my absence, my heartbeat and blood pressure had returned to normal.

After that experience, I not only felt my work more deeply, but my work intensified because I was more committed to taking care of myself. I continued giving energizations, but in a more reasonable fashion, relying on Mauricio to guide me. To this day he is with me each time I work. I feel his presence and that of other light beings very powerfully. It makes my own presence stronger and opens my expression of Spirit even more. It magnifies my love and strengthens the incredible feeling I receive when I am giving. I am everything and I am nothing. I am infinite humility. I am the channel through which light and energy are transferred from one part of God to another. I know the person lying on the table is an extension of God, a piece of that very same Light. There is no question in my mind. I know it absolutely. I can feel it, just as I can feel Mauricio's presence in the room with me.

Sometimes, Mauricio's presence is stronger than at other times. I remember one particular week when he was extremely strong, and paranormal events were occurring often, to the delight of the students at Delphi. It was shortly after I began giving energizations regularly, and Patricia and Marshall had decided to give them as a gift to each of the students who took the Healing Mysteries class. Its purpose was to initiate them into their next step of development. At the time, my sons Marshall and Patrick were ten and nine years old and had taken on the same role I used to perform for Mauricio. They led the client into the sanctuary and asked them to lie on the table. They began their work by relaxing the client, touching their third eye to balance the male and female energies, and speaking mantras in Portuguese. Although I didn't know it at the time, they finished by gently kissing the person on the forehead before leaving the room. This was their gift to the people.

As soon as you walked into my home, you could feel the crisp, electrical energy. Our healing sanctuary fairly crackled with charged current. The moment I began the student energizations, unusual things began to happen. Many of them saw huge sparks of lights in their heads during their sessions, and others saw lights actually flash out from the walls of the sanctuary. Through all of it, one man in the class remained skeptical, but was intrigued by all the excitement in the group. He came to my home and was waiting his turn in the small room outside the sanctuary, when a huge spark of light flashed from the ceiling and out of the wall over the man's head. He ducked, looking sheepishly up to see if any more lights were coming. They didn't. So he hesitantly entered the sanctuary and lay on the table. It was my son Marshall's turn to prepare him, and as he began, the room slowly brightened until it was dimly lit with a subtle orange glow that seemed to emanate from the walls.

Marshall had seen Mauricio bring light many times, so the phenomenon of the glowing orange lights was not particularly surprising to him, although he did look around the room somewhat nervously. He went on with his duties, and as he stood at the man's head, his attention was attracted to a vaporous cloud emanating from the statue of Mother Mary at the foot of the table. As he watched, the statue itself changed shape and he saw Mauricio emerge from it. At first, Marshall just stood and watched. But as Mauricio's energy grew larger and began to move towards him, he became frightened, thinking that Mauricio wanted to incorporate his body. He quickly left the sanctuary and ran to tell me what happened. He said, "Mommy, I saw Papa. He was coming towards me. I wasn't scared of him, but I'm not ready for that yet!" I didn't feel it was Mauricio's intention to incorporate Marshall, and I assured him that he had nothing to worry about. Marshall is open and sensitive, and maybe that is why it happened. I loved feeling Mauricio's presence in the room with me. He had a way of electrifying the air.

In 1995, two years after Mauricio's death, I accompanied Patricia and Marshall on their annual trip to Lily Dale, an old and very famous spiritualist retreat in upstate New York, not far from Niagara Falls. Patricia and Marshall were presenters there, and were giving weeklong classes. I was scheduled to give energizations and to assist them with their teaching. The atmosphere at Lily Dale is quite special and unique. Spiritual and psychic energy abounds there, and every healing, reading or energization seems to be much more intense, much more powerful than normal. By coincidence (or perhaps not) we were there on July 28th, the date of our wedding anniversary, when Mauricio and I were married in Brasilia.

I woke up that day feeling melancholic. I had a strong desire to see Mauricio. For some unknown reason, that day's schedule of energizations became terribly mixed up, and I ended up completely rearranging the morning schedule, moving some clients' appointments by as much as two hours. This rescheduling affected the afternoon appointments as well. One man who had been scheduled to come early in the afternoon was moved to the last appointment of the day. Everything proceeded unremarkably until that last appointment. This client was an older gentleman who entered and lay down on the table. As I began working on him, I began to feel an overwhelming sense of love filling the room. But since this happens often, I didn't think it was unusual until the feeling of love intensified so much that

I knew this to be anything but usual. As I moved from his head to his feet, the reason I was feeling these overwhelming waves of love became clear.

As I approached the man's side, I looked down at him in shock at what I saw. I was completely bewildered. I just couldn't believe what I was seeing. This was not the same man who had laid down a few moments before. There lying upon the table was Mauricio! I could see him so vividly. His eyes were closed and his face exuded a radiant glow of warm light that seemed to fill his body with a deep peace. His white silken hair lay softly back upon his head. My first impulse was to reach out and touch him. It was all I could do not to take him into my arms. And although I had seen many unusual and extraordinary things in my life, I had never seen anything like this. Seeing Mauricio incorporated in this man's body took me totally by surprise. It was the last thing I would have expected, particularly since Mauricio had never been fond of or even comfortable with the subject of incorporation.

A thousand feelings flooded through me. I had felt so close to Mauricio in so many ways since he had left. I had even seen his presence here, there and everywhere. But never like this! I was being given the most magnificent gift from spirit and was having a very difficult time handling it. I didn't know what to do except to continue doing what I was doing. So I continued to work. Only now it was Mauricio on the table on whom I was working.

At one point the energy was so fused I didn't know who was giving and who was receiving! As much as I was giving, I was receiving ten fold. My emotional self kept getting in the way. I wanted to embrace him and tell him how much I loved him. I could feel him feeling the same. Our connection was as strong as it had always been. My mind began to reel, and my thoughts kicked in. Thought, that great killer of psychic and mystical experience. I began to think that this couldn't possibly be Mauricio lying here on the table, even though my heart knew it was. I wanted to preserve my professional demeanor, but I didn't want to lose this opportunity to be with my love. In the end my logical, professional self won out and I continued on with the energization. I finished the session, and left the room briefly to compose myself. I told him to stay there with his eyes closed until I returned.

I was only gone about five minutes. When I returned the older gentleman had already gotten off the table and was sitting on the sofa staring in a trance-like state, his body trembling. When we looked at each other I knew he was deeply moved by his experience. He was unable to speak, and so was I. We just looked at each other for what felt like an eternity. We had shared an incredible and sacred experience, but neither of us could find any words for it. We didn't really feel the need. We just smiled and hugged each other, and I never hugged anyone after energization. As he was walking out the door, he whispered in my ear that he had a message for me, one he would tell me tomorrow. Then he left.

The next morning at the conference I saw him again. He brought me a three-page letter and a picture he had drawn of his experience. I sat quietly and listened as he told me about the picture. He had deeply relaxed on the table and had concentrated on his breathing. Soon, he felt himself floating above the earth. A man came to him, greeted him and took him further upward to a pure, divine place in which he was surrounded by nature. Here he met and walked with an energy he knew to be the Christ. He had never felt so safe and secure and at peace in his entire life. He trusted completely what had happened. His eyes spoke to me the magnitude of his feelings. It was a beautiful experience that neither of us will ever forget.

Then he gave me the letter and told me that it was my message. It was written in pigeon English, and as I read the words, I immediately recognized whom it was from. Mauricio's broken English was captured in the letter's phrasing and sentence construction, even including his trademark "more than possible." At the end, the letter said, "Remember, my love, that you are my Neika and will always be my Neika." My logical mind was at work again. Only this time I reasoned that there was no way that this man could have known any of this. And even if he spoke or wrote English like a Brasilian, he could never have known my spiritual name, a name that was shared only with Mauricio.

I was elated. I was so grateful to this man for sharing the purity of his heart and this incredible gift with me. He too was exhilarated by the experience. After sharing this story with the group at the conference, we had our picture taken together. I expressed my gratitude and said that I would always love him. Later, I tried to contact him again, but couldn't find him. I tried the address on the conference list, but it didn't exist. I asked several people in the New York area to try to find him, but they couldn't find a trace. I don't know where he went, or even if he was of this world. But I am still grateful to him for this extraordinary experience.

On the drive home from Lily Dale, I was charged! I was filled with passion! I felt so alive! I could feel my molecules, atoms and cells, and the kinship they shared, all vibrating harmoniously. I felt the synchronicity. I could hear words being said seconds before they came out of Patricia or Marshall's mouth. Patricia was responsive to the energy and was uplifted just being in it. We had been looking at each other a short while when she said to me, "Kimberly, it is time you began to teach this gift." The words that came out of her mouth were in a man's voice! She wasn't aware of this, but I was shocked, both at the tone of her voice and at what she suggested, although her ideas never ceased to amaze me. At first I felt resistance. I wasn't sure how I could possibly teach this energization technique. The concept seemed too advanced for most people. But I learned from a master who showed me the way. He was a true example, and this is what he gave me, the confidence to know that I had something special to share with others.

I started to think about the fact that I was only one person. I realized how many more could be touched and lifted spiritually by this sacred experience, if there were others channeling this light too. How could I deny them the experience of becoming pioneers of light, bringing Spirit into matter so that God's love and presence could be better sustained in the world? If the spiritual growth of hundreds, even thousands, could be enhanced by this light and energy flowing through them, then how could I withhold Mauricio's healing methods, or fail to share his experiences. I thought about it all the way back from Lily Dale. The more I did, the more I felt that it was a logical next step, the next piece of the puzzle that allowed me to fulfill my purpose. We talked about it all the way back to Delphi, and by the time we arrived, not only had I made the commitment to do it, but we had already outlined how the material would be structured. There was no way all of the material could be taught in one class, so we decided to teach it in two. My Papa Marshall and I would work together.

14

The energy, the faith, the devotion which we
bring to this endeavor will light our country
and all who serve it, and the glow from that
fire can truly light the world.

–John Fitgerald Kennedy

BACK AT DELPHI, we set to work. We developed the Spiritual
Anatomy and Energization I and II classes together. Marshall
stretches the minds of the students, teaching the Spiritual
Anatomy, while I stretch their energy, teaching them energization. By
working through both parts of the process, the student is able to
reach the point at which they can sustain the higher energies of Spirit
in their bodies for an extended period.

Student initiates must learn how to lift their own energy to the
highest place imaginable. They must reach the place in their hearts
where they truly feel that they are bringing and sustaining God's
goodness here on earth. In order to bring through this cosmic energy and light during energization, they must know, with absolute conviction, that they are part of God. It is their energy and their intention
that helps to lift the consciousness of the person lying on the table,
and they must be able to sustain that sacred and spiritual energy for
the entire session. It is always a test for the initiate because he or she
must evoke the energies of light through his words of conviction.

The initiates who reach this point truly understand that there is no
separation between and among humans, between humans and God,
and that all things around us, including ourselves, are all expressions
of God. They come to know, deep in their hearts, that our human
perception of separation, of separateness, is only an illusion. They tap
into God's absolute and universal love, and come to a lasting realization and a true understanding of the sacredness of each and every

existence, whether it appears on its surface to be positive or negative. Mauricio once told me that when he met Sai Baba, he told him in a somewhat boisterous voice, "You are not God." Sai Baba only looked at him and replied, "The only difference between you and me is that I know that I am, and you don't." This bothered Mauricio for some time. He had felt the truth about what Sai Baba had said to him. Mauricio's own sense of unworthiness in life had sometimes left him feeling empty and separate from God, and he knew that a part of himself was now being healed.

One of the special people who have reached this point of understanding is Lorraine Tabor. From a humble spiritual beginning, Lorraine's experiences drew her ever more deeply into her current spiritual reality. They began with her first energization from Mauricio at Lily Dale in 1992. During that session, Lorraine says she really wasn't able to relax, but for days afterward, she felt as though her forehead was indented over her third eye, and she smelled the fragrance of roses everywhere she went. The experience so inspired Lorraine that she eventually came to Delphi and continued her spiritual studies. After completing the prerequisites, Lorraine arrived to take the first Spiritual Anatomy and Energization class ever offered. On the first day of class, she and the other students received Energization Initiation from me. Later, Lorraine shared her experience with me. She told me that the very essence of her being, every atom was awakening to the purpose of working with Mauricio and the light. She could feel in some strange way that she was being prepared for her next step.

During the session, Lorraine felt extreme warmth from her knees to her waist, as though her legs were sunburned. She felt pressure in each of her chakras, most intensely in the solar plexus, throat and third eye charkas. A lighted triangle emanated from her third eye as a golden spiral opened and emerged from her crown chakra. At the end of the session, she heard angels and celestial beings of light join in the singing of Ave Maria, and she was filled with ecstasy. She was very emotional afterward and wrote in her notebook that the session "awakened me to the true knowing of the I AM that I AM, in the midst of my doubt and fears. It made me truly aware of the true sacredness and oneness of all things, and deepened my awareness of light, love and other dimensions." When I had finished her session and Lorraine got up from the table to return to her seat, she physically saw a big ball of blue light to my left, a bit bigger than a basketball. This, she felt, was Uhr. Afterwards, Lorraine's class went to the Healing Sanctuary to practice on each other what they had learned. For Lorraine, it seemed as though her hands had sensors in them. She didn't need to look with her physical eyes because her hands could "see, sense and feel" everything.

During the class, a number of students became discouraged at the task of learning and remembering all there was to learn about giving energizations. Lorraine later wrote to tell me that it was only the incredible patience, guidance and love Marshall and I showed that carried them through. This kept their hearts open so that they could learn and gain confidence in their abilities. By the time Saturday evening came along, each of these student initiates successfully gave an energization for the first time to a stranger. Lorraine completed her studies at Delphi and now runs her own spiritual healing ministry. If I ever needed confirmation that teaching Mauricio's energization process to others was the right step, Lorraine's experiences provided it. In a recent letter, Lorraine described some of her own experiences during energization:

"When I first started doing energizations I was very mental, going through the process and trying not to leave anything out. Now I am more relaxed and am a better conduit for the energía. During the preparatory phase I can feel my crown open and a flow of energy, heat, love and peace enter into me. My body becomes very warm and my hands intensely warm and sensitive. I truly feel the client is my own brother or sister. It causes me to feel very humble and allows the energies to flow easily.

"When I call upon Master Jesus and others to join me I can feel their presence. With my eyes closed I often see little lights at this time. There are numerous times when I call for them that I am overwhelmed with incredible chills. From discussions with clients, I have discovered that they are also aware of and truly experiencing the Christ energy at that time, and for some it is quite an emotional experience. It is often a very emotional experience for me, too. Many times I traveled into different dimensions while doing energizations. A few times, when I called 'energía, força, etc.,' the voice that came out was not mine.

"Some clients say they feel like they are being lifted off the table during energization, and in one particular case I watched it happen. I had just finished and stepped back to leave the woman in her experience a bit longer when her arms rose up ever so slowly as if she was embracing someone. Then, her whole body began to lift up, off the table. I was shocked and scared. When the session was over, the woman said she was lifted off the table and was moving toward Christ. After this experience, the woman looked ten years younger. Even her friends commented on her appearance for days afterwards.

"In a recent energization, I was doing the circles over a client's chakras when, with my physical eyes, I saw a ball of light opposite me about eight feet away. It was about three or four inches in diameter, white with a faint blue outline. I don't know how long it was there but it vanished just after I noticed it.

"One night, I was working on my friend Jane when in the middle of the session, her eyes opened wide and she had a look of astonishment. I thought to myself, 'What could be wrong?' but continued with the healing. After the session she said, 'You didn't tell me anyone else was going to be here.' She described a man she had seen participating in the healing and as she described him, 'I knew without a doubt that it was Mauricio.'

"It is most humbling and such a blessing to be able to serve as an instrument in such a sacred process, to be able to bring through such light, love and healing energy to others, to be an instrument in their awakening and transformation, and to be in the presence of The Blessed Ones of Light. I am most grateful to be able to serve Spirit in this capacity and I am grateful to you for sharing this beautiful process. It is with a much, much, much deeper awareness and understanding I close with these words:

"In Love and Light, Lorraine."

Another unique colleague of mine to have completed Spiritual Anatomy and Energization is Ed Aguilar. Ed has incorporated energization into his own healing ministry that also includes massage, cleansings in the tradition of the Curanderos of Mexico, plus some Native American Ceremonies such as the Sweats, and Vision Quest. In putting together the material for this book, I asked Ed to tell me about his experience, which I know was very inspiring to him:

"My first experience with 'Brasilian Energization' was during the initiation you gave me at Delphi. That experience was my opening into the cosmic universe that I knew was deep within me—I just didn't know how to open the door.

"You began by asking me to breathe with you. You held my hand and we became one. Then you began a guided meditation and I saw I was on the path of a very bright light that appeared to me as the Sun. I did not feel intense heat from this light, but instead the most incredible sense of unconditional love. The intense light turned into a subtler, bright yellow light and Jesus seemed to step out of that light. I realized that He was the light.

"I was on a path of light that led to where he was standing and as I approached, he put his hands together and a ball of yellow light came directly at me and entered my heart chakra. Words cannot express what I actually felt at that moment, but it was closest to a very intense feeling of unconditional love. I had a sense of 'knowing,' as if I understood everything in the universe. Then I felt you call me back.

"Before I started my journey back, I looked at Jesus once more and I thought I heard Him say, 'Rise from the dead,' or 'You can rise from the dead' or something to that effect. He held a white dove in His hand that appeared to be dead, but as he cupped one hand over the other and breathed on the dove, it awakened and flew away. Then He vanished. However, there was a cross on the palm of both my hands. Then I was back and you asked if I was okay. I couldn't find the words to tell you what I had just experienced. Was it an awakening, or was it something more meaningful or something more symbolic? I am on the path to find out.

"After that initiation I made up my mind that I would not leave Delphi without experiencing an energization from you. I did not know what to expect, but made up my mind to be as open as I could be. That night, several of us entered your home, which was so very calm. You could hear Kodoish playing and the music wafted down the stairs and calmed us as we waited. When it was finally my turn for the long-awaited experience, I think you sensed my apprehension, excitement and soothed me merely by asking how I was. You told me to lie on the table, relax, and take deep breaths. Then you began connecting to my energy. As you began your prayers, my journey began.

"I quickly found myself experiencing different colors of light and cosmic beings all around me. I couldn't see faces, just light emanating from all of the beings. They all were speaking at the same time: some in English, others in languages I could not understand. All were teaching me about my path.

"I felt like I was traveling through different levels of cosmic light and there was no end to this beautiful vast cosmic ocean of stars and light and waves of energy. I felt every wavelength of this energy and could feel my physical self begin to melt away for it seemed that I was shaking myself out of my body. The different colored lights were shooting inside me like lightning bolts and I could feel an omnipresence of pure unconditional love. I felt like my whole self was awakening to the Spirit of being. I still cannot find the words to describe all the sensations.

"I heard Kimberly call for Shallar, Enoch, Akron, Jesus, and other cosmic beings, and then I saw Mother Mary and heard her say, 'Everything in its own time' I could sense the presence of Mauricio, his hands removing excess and negative energy from me as he prayed in Portuguese. Then there was a calm and I felt myself return to my body. Then, as you brought me back to this reality, you told me to move slowly to allow my body to adjust to the energization. Afterwards we briefly discussed my experience but I still had no words that could truly describe what I had just experienced.

"That was my first energization, but not my last. I decided that I would learn and could learn to do this energization. I took the Spiritual Anatomy and Energization classes and used the 'Brasilian Energization' technique with family and friends before actually using it on clients. But it did not take me long to incorporate it into my practice.

"I would like to tell you about an experience I had with one of my clients. I will refer to her as Helene. Helene first came to me for the 'Egg Cleansing,' to clean the etheric body of negative energy. During the cleansing, I noticed that her energy was very low and discovered that her chakras were not balanced and there were other physical abnormalities. I discussed the energization technique with her and asked if she was open to receiving this procedure. She agreed.

"The day of the energization, Helene came early. I asked her to lie on the table and relax, and I turned on the Kodoish music. After about five minutes of relaxation, I began my connection and the energization. It was difficult to get her energy to move up from the base chakra, but once this was done the energy moved faster. When I called the cosmic beings of light, I felt a strong shift in her energy as well as my own and knew she was starting to travel out of her body. At that point it became difficult for me to concentrate on the next step, as I felt the urge to travel with her, but somehow the prayers pulled me back and I continued with the energization.

"When I finished, I sat down with an extreme feeling of unconditional love for Helene. After we discussed the process and compared notes, Helene thanked me profusely, telling me that the energization had been the most Spiritual experience she had ever had in her sixty years. A few months later Helene told me in a letter that she believed she received a new gift from God, me. She wrote, 'I originally learned of the Brasilian healer Mauricio Panisset from a spiritual teacher and author, Wayne Dyer. Wayne met Mauricio and described the healing saying how Mauricio was calling "energía, energía" when he was calling upon the light. I wanted very much to meet Mauricio Panisset. I prayed to God to meet him, or someone like him. Can you imagine this? The circle is closed now. You were a gift from God sent to me in Mauricio's place. I remember how sad I was when I learned that Mauricio passed. Again, God has His own ways and His own timing. Everything materializes for us at the time we are ready.'"

I have been blessed to know each and every one of the dedicated healers who are committed to bringing light to the world through Mauricio's energization healing techniques. Many, such as Lorraine Tabor and Ed Aguilar, have had incredible experiences themselves while doing so, and their experiences vary as much as they do. Each one shows that human beings can indeed bring Spirit into matter. Bringing Spirit into matter can be as small as stroking a pet with love, or as large as bringing God's light energy into another human being. The activity doesn't really matter. It's only a matter of degree. Practicing tolerance toward the person who cuts you off in traffic brings love into your consciousness instead of hate. Smiling at the clerk who is rude creates love in that moment instead of anger. Seemingly insignificant acts contribute to a greater sense of love in the world. Maybe your smile will affect that clerk and he will be pleasant to his customers for the rest of the day. It's the little subtle acts of love we do that bring God closer to humanity.

But as humans, we forget or we don't know. No matter how spiritual we feel, we still have the feeling of separation sometimes, the feeling that God is outside of us rather than within, and that He is smiting us rather than smiling upon us. That feeling keeps us from shining our light here on earth. When you need help in life, call upon spiritual help and have faith that you are being listened to by the invisible forces that help us all the time. Call upon the masters, the angels, the archangels, Jesus and Mother Mary. Call upon your relatives or others you know who have made their transition. If you feel you want to call on Mauricio, call his spiritual name Akron three times and he will help you. If you don't feel anything, ask for confirmation, and then be open to receive a sign. Be ready to recognize a "coincidence" in your life, and then follow the guidance of your heart. Ask to know and to feel the light within you, and trust that help will follow.

Spiritual work is not only about our own individual growth and evolution. Its greater purpose is to open greater dimensions of God's Love and Light upon the earth. As we are able to heal ourselves, we make it that much easier for others to follow. We create a bridge and a pathway that serve as a roadmap for others. For each of us who rise up, the consciousness of all becomes elevated, and the seeker is aided by the efforts of those who have come before him. By helping ourselves and others, we assist all. The one contributes to the whole. Just as the Christ showed the way for us, each of us can lead the way for others. And the more we open to these higher dimensions, the greater our ability to sustain the light and collectively move into a higher energy. This is the ultimate goal, to raise human consciousness into higher consciousness. My mother says it best when she says to students, "The only eyes, the only hands, and the only heart God has on earth are yours and mine."

15

Truth resides in every human heart, and one
has to search for it there and to be guided by
truth as one sees it.

—Mahatma Gandhi

I TOLD MAURICIO MANY times that his healing work would
continue long after he was gone. Little did I know it would be
through the many people that I trained to do energization. I
knew someday I would write or help to write a book about this man
of light, and I told him so. In typical fashion Mauricio would always
say, "Ah, Kimberly, I don't care about a book."

Still, I always said, "But Mauricio, you should care about this
book. Through the book others will learn from you. They will experience the trials, tribulations and struggles you went through spiritually. Each person will recognize your spiritual strengths as well as your
human frailties. And because of you, they will feel better about themselves and the conflicts they too may be feeling within about spiritual matters. You will inspire them to know that God truly does exist,
and that he works through ordinary people like you, and me, and
them. And through your story they too will be inspired to make a
connection with their own spirit, so that they too can bring through
a greater dimension of love and healing into all aspects of their lives."
He never said anything more, but I knew he was touched that I cared
enough to want to tell his story.

Many saw and experienced Mauricio's light, but still they didn't
believe. They couldn't believe even after seeing. Mauricio was well
aware that there would always be those who would never understand
him or his gift. It was beyond their comprehension. Mauricio
explained to me that some people had not opened their minds suffi-

ciently enough to even store the experience. They had no reference point. Therefore, they couldn't possibly accept what they had just witnessed. In cases like these, his light could cause more disruption than help in their lives.

One day, a few years after Mauricio died, my mother handed me the book *People in the Attic* by Doretta Johnson. Patricia and her colleague William Roll, a psychic researcher, had met Doretta during a psychic investigation of her home for a television show. Even before I read the book, I knew I had to call her. It wasn't like me to call a stranger out of the blue, but I was compelled. I didn't know why, but something told me that Doretta and I should meet.

I called Doretta and introduced myself. I didn't want her to think I was crazy, so I explained why I was calling. I told her I didn't know what it was that we were meant to accomplish together, but I was sure that there was something. I went on to tell her about my late husband, Mauricio Panisset, who had a gift of light, and that maybe she would be the one to help me write the book about him. I was also open to the possibility that our meeting may not have anything to do with the book at all, and told her that no matter the reason, I felt strongly that we were supposed to be in each other's lives.

Doretta is very gifted psychically. Although she was surprised to hear from me, she felt the truth in what I was saying and told me to come to Indiana right away. Before I went, I sat down and read her book cover to cover. I was blown away by the incredible events that occurred to her and her family, and the honesty and emotion she expressed in sharing her story, *People in the Attic* is about the experiences of the Johnson family with the many poltergeists and psychic phenomena that transpired over many years in their house, an old hotel. She tells about her search to understand what was happening to them and why. Doretta also experienced light phenomena similar to Mauricio's.

After I read her book I was convinced that, because of her own experiences, she could both understand and write about Mauricio. It took a lot of courage to write the truth about what happened to her. How many would believe a story like hers, of poltergeists, hauntings, and other phenomena? It gave me hope for telling my own story. I didn't know if she had the desire to write another book, or whether she would agree to write mine. All I knew was that I had to meet her and find out.

Three days later, I arrived at her house. Doretta's home was full of psychic energy. You could feel it immediately, the moment you walked in the door. I felt entities everywhere. It was as if her home was a portal or doorway to the other side. It was intense. Even though we were total strangers, Doretta's energy felt very familiar to me and mine to her. It was as if we had found a lost part of ourselves that had been missing for a long time. Although we felt an instant rapport, we both silently wondered why I was there. That evening, we were in the kitchen preparing dinner together when I picked up a spoon to stir the mashed potatoes. The spoon went soft and wilted in my hand. It didn't faze either of us. I was used to Mauricio melting forks and spoons, and Doretta was used to phenomena occurring constantly in her house. So we just looked at each other and laughed, brushing it off. I took the potatoes to the table and went back for the vegetables, but as I picked up a spoon to stir the vegetables, it too melted in my hand. I just looked at her and said, "Is this confirmation?"

Doretta didn't answer, but since Mauricio's trademark was melted silverware, I believed it was a confirmation to me that she was meant to write the book. I took it as a sign that I was in the right place, and doing the right thing. I went to bed that night feeling more at ease, and knew that everything would fall into place, in time. I trusted that I was there for the right reasons and they would be revealed to me as I needed them.

Doretta had been asking for confirmation too. When she woke up the next morning and walked out of her bedroom, she was brought to her knees as a wave of love swept through the hallway filling her with the most incredible tenderness she had ever felt. She began to cry uncontrollably. She sensed Mauricio's presence with her, and could feel the depth of love he had for me. She had never felt love like that in her entire life and didn't know it was even possible to experience that kind of love here on earth. This was her confirmation.

When I found her crying in the hallway, she told me what had happened. I went back into my room and got a videotape of Mauricio doing an energization. We went to the living room and laid down to watch the film. We held hands and just relaxed into the energy. As we lay there watching, we saw Mauricio's energy slowly emanate from the TV and hover over Doretta. As his spirit floated above her, a smoky film began to ooze out of her solar plexus. For twenty minutes we watched motionless and in silence. I didn't know what to make of this. I only knew it was significant. It was only later that Doretta explained it to me, and I understood. She told me about the cysts in her right breast, and that she had been scheduled to have the cysts removed surgically. But without knowing why, she had inexplicably canceled the surgery only two weeks before. She told me that when Mauricio was above her, she felt the cysts in her breast break up and dissolve. The smoke that we saw was the remnants of the now dissolved cysts moving out of her body.

I was impressed at her sensitivity and her ability to receive Mauricio's energy. I assumed it was because she was so open. I thought that this was a great beginning to our work together, and we spent the next two weeks at her house while she asked me questions about myself and my life with Mauricio. I was sharing parts of myself that I had not shared with anyone since his death. I didn't know I had that many tears left, but as I talked, my wounding over his death was beginning to heal.

In telling my story to Doretta, I learned so much about myself. I discovered that my life with Mauricio had helped me mature spiritually, and it had vastly broadened the depth of my capacity to give and receive love. And for the first time, I also recognized how I had closed myself off from the possibility of ever allowing love in my life again. I had convinced myself that you only experience that kind of love once in a lifetime. How could I ever love another so deeply as I did Mauricio? But one morning while lying in bed, I felt an overwhelming desire to know this kind of love again. My heart fluttered at the possibility. I was inspired at the very idea. It had been three years, and for the first time, my heart was once again open. I sent my love out into the universe, asking love to find me once more. I knew I was healing and I felt a great peace settle over me.

The next day I shared my feelings with Doretta, excited to think that I could actually open to the possibility of love anew, as scary as it seemed. She just looked at me for a moment, and then smiled with a knowing look. She said that earlier that morning, as she and I stood talking in the hallway, she'd had a vision of the man with whom I would spend the rest of my life. She saw the man I would marry bending down to tie his shoe, and she knew that he was preparing to meet me. She said that neither he nor I would recognize each other at first, and that he would step in and out of my energy several times before we did. A feeling of shock and fear flooded through me. I didn't know if I was quite ready to hear that. But when she said it, chills went coursing through my body. I could feel her truth, and that scared me even more. She told me I would meet him in six months. I was not quite ready to embrace the thought of another man in my life, even though I had just asked for it. So I managed to put it out of my mind and focused instead on the book.

I returned to Doretta's three more times to work on the book. But as often happens, my relationship with Doretta turned out differently from what we thought. Sometimes you think that you are headed towards one purpose, or that a certain person has been put into your life for a specific reason, but it turns out to be something very different that what you had imagined. This was the case with Doretta. We discovered that we were actually mirrors for each other. Our friendship and love helped heal the feminine part of our broken hearts. My healing occurred when reliving my life with Mauricio and sharing the depth of my soul and all its agony. I reclaimed that part of myself that was lost when I lost Mauricio. I was free to love again.

Doretta's healing had two parts. Because she spent most of her life believing that the gift of light that came from her hands was evil, she tried to hide it, even from herself. No one had ever helped her to understand. After we met she discovered that she too had a gift for healing. This discovery led to the belief that her light could be used for good, and that it truly was a gift from God. Doretta's healing also involved a new path. She was feeling a pressing need to release duty from her life and replace it with love. This feeling had progressed to the point where she realized she needed to change her life. She needed time for herself, and realized she was unable to write my book. Although I understood, I was at a loss. The book would not be written the way I expected, and I was heartbroken. I was discouraged, thinking that Mauricio's story might not ever be told. And I was still too resistant to think I could write it myself.

I took charge, and decided that if Doretta wasn't the one to write it, it must be someone else. And I began to search for that someone else. Within a month I asked several others to write the book, and each time I was turned down for one reason or another. Discouraged and frustrated, I'd had enough. I decided not to even think about the book for a while. So I put away all of my papers and notes, all of my interviews with Doretta, and all of the tapes of our conversations. But even though I put all the materials away, Mauricio's book never left my mind. I had made a promise to him that I would tell his story, and I would get it done, one way or another. My work with Doretta had brought the healing I needed, and helped me to recall the many feelings, emotions and events of my life. Doretta is more of a sister than a friend. She is a part of me. To this day, if she is sad, I feel it. When she experiences trauma, I know it. There are times when her presence is with me for weeks on end, and I always send her my love and support. I still held fast to my faith and the knowledge that there are no accidents. When it was time to write the book, it would happen.

I put the past year on the back burner and went on with my life, renewing my commitment to Spirit and to my boys. I worked a great deal of the time, teaching at Delphi University, and traveling throughout the country giving energizations. Months went by. Patricia, Marshall and I traveled to Vienna to work with a group. We had been invited to the Metaphysical Center of Vienna by our friend and colleague Helen Descovich, the founder of the center. On the last night of our stay, one of my clients, an opera singer named Shake Kazajian, invited me out for dinner. As we sat at the table talking, she looked into my eyes and with a deep conviction said, "Kimberly, I just saw the man with whom you will spend the rest of your life." My mouth dropped open. A thousand feelings flooded through me, but I just looked at her, stunned. "No, really," she said in a matter of fact way, "It's as clear as day. You will meet him within six months." Still unbelieving, I recovered my composure. I laughed and told her it wasn't going to happen. Doretta had said the same thing nearly four months ago, and her prediction hadn't come true, at least not yet. With a smile, I told Shake that if she was right, I would fly her to America to sing Ave Maria at my wedding!

I went to bed that night feeling a desire for love. During the night I dreamt I had just finished working at a big convention and was worried that I wasn't going to get to the airport on time to make it to my next job. I left the building and hailed a taxi. I said to the driver, "What am I going to do? I'm late and I'm going to miss my plane!" The taxi driver said, "No, it's all right, you aren't going to miss it, its all waiting for you." He loaded my luggage into the back and we left the airport. We drove to the intersection of two highways, where a 747 was waiting. The taxi driver turned to me and said, "You see, I told you, it waited for you." He escorted me to the plane. Then, out of the blue, another man appeared. He embraced me in his arms, and then looked deeply into my eyes and told me that he was waiting for me. Although I could see his face clearly, I did not recognize him. I only recognized what I saw in his eyes, eyes that seemed so very familiar to me. He then escorted me onto the plane, and said goodbye. Then he was gone.

For whatever reason, that dream had an impact on me. I wasn't sure what it meant, but I woke up feeling alive and hopeful, peaceful and invigorated. I thought to myself how incredible it would be to find love again. I wondered what it would be like to love another, to love another as deeply as I did Mauricio. Could I ever settle for less? I returned home with an inner peace and an even greater sense of devotion to my work and my children. Gone were the thoughts of "what if" and replacing them was an absolute acceptance of whatever the future held in store.

The next few months were the happiest for me since Mauricio died. I was content with myself, with the life I had created, and wherever I was going next, even though I didn't know exactly where that was. But I knew I was on the right track. My clarity and perspective were in order and my life became consistent. I was teaching and giving energizations. Everything was clearer than it had ever been before. I was okay, and I was doing the work I loved. Everything else was in God's hands. I was concentrating on my work at Delphi.

16

Man is never so tall as when he kneels before
God—never so great as when he humbles
himself before God. And the man who kneels
to God can stand up to anything.

–Louis H. Evans

OUR "DELPHI" HAS been called one of the best-kept
secrets in the world. Delphi was founded by my mom,
Patricia Hayes, and has developed over the past thirty-five
years, since I was seven. A white water river wraps around our school
that is nestled in and surrounded by nature. We're not easy to find,
but if you are meant to be here, you will be. On the map we are
where Georgia, Tennessee, and North Carolina come together, outside of the little Town of McCaysville, Georgia. The Cherokee
Nation held their tribal conclaves here, and it was to the natural
springs that flow here that they brought their sick and dying for
healing.

Delphi is an experience beyond a place. Stepping onto the grounds
brings a rush of energy to the head and the heart. Within minutes
you have the unexplainable feeling you have come home. It doesn't
matter how many times you have come and gone, you always feel it.

Something is different here, something unworldly, yet solid. It is
hard to put into words. When people come, I watch day to day as
their judgments fall away. Their curiosity mounts as they open more
and more. Their worries and problems slide easily to the background
as they settle in. I know that most of them have been drawn by an
inner stirring, and have come with a similar intent. But my greatest
reward is seeing them connect with Spirit and the transformation that
occurs. For years I have watched people come to Delphi for many different reasons, yet all have the same purpose: to improve their lives,

gain greater knowledge of Spirit, and to develop their spiritual abilities in order to help themselves and others.

Delphi is known for its certification programs in Metaphysical Healing and RoHun spiritual psychotherapy. But first and foremost, Delphi is a mystery school, where esoteric knowledge has been preserved and taught only to serious seekers. Some students begin their intuitive and spiritual training with the program, Connecting With Spirit. Others, who already know they want to use their abilities to help people, go directly to the In-depth Channeling course, affectionately known as "boot camp," an intensive week that teaches them to open their psychic channels and use their spiritual abilities. Those who complete the program receive certification as intuitive counselors. Students who complete the full course of study can earn certification as a Doctor of Metaphysics, a Doctor of RoHun, or both. Channels and healers trained at Delphi share their light and healing in their own spiritual practices all over the world.

Many visitors come to Delphi for the Mauricio Panisset Healing Sanctuary and Service held on the first Friday of each month. When he was alive, Mauricio spent a great deal of his time here giving healings. He and his Brother Lights have markedly increased the energy field here. I loved being outside of the sanctuary while Mauricio worked inside. The sanctuary itself is an octagonal building with six skylights located in the roof. One could stand outside the sanctuary and watch as light flashed from all of the skylights, dancing as it passed through the windows to light up the night sky. And sometimes, other lights would come flashing too, as if they were all communicating together. Lights could be seen at Delphi even when Mauricio wasn't working. To this day, people still experience phenomena in the teaching halls, sometimes in class, and in their quiet walks in nature. Mauricio's spirit continues to provide awakening, light healing and phenomena to all of those who are searching.

Late one afternoon in August, I had just finished an energization for a student. Because I was teaching that night, I planned to drive him back to the school myself. I left the student, a man in his late forties, downstairs in my living room while I went upstairs to get ready for class. When I came back, ready to leave, I found him sitting on the floor with Patrick and Marshall, one boy under each arm, helping them with their homework. It seemed so natural. I got chills, but easily brushed it off and thought no more about it. I was in a hurry to get back to school and was already focused on teaching class that night.

A week later when the class ended, I was there to say good-bye to everyone, when that same student, Charles Curcio, walked over to me. He said, "I know this is going to sound crazy but I feel the need to tell you this. A few months ago, a psychic described to me the woman she said I would spend the rest of my life with. And I think it's you." As he spoke, I got chills once more. But for some reason his statement didn't even faze me and I said, very naturally and casually, "Well, that's funny, because six months ago in Vienna, a woman told me I would meet the man I would spend the rest of my life with at Delphi this month!" We both laughed. We had said these things lightly, as if it was no big deal, and we continued to chat for a few minutes more.

As the airport van pulled up, Charles and I said goodbye. When he hugged me, I felt drawn to him. When he let go of me, he looked into my eyes and said simply, "I have some things I have to take care of." Again, I thought nothing of it, but just before he climbed into the van to leave, he turned and looked back at me as I looked back at him. I froze. My heart sank. I recognized those eyes! But whose eyes were they? I didn't know. But what I did know was that this was not our first good-bye. We had said farewell before. As the van drove away, I stood motionless in the road for what felt like an eternity. "What was that all about?" I asked myself. Finally, I drove home. That night I was in bed at 8:30 and slept the whole night through, the first time I was able to do that in the four years since Mauricio died.

I didn't hear from Charles again for a few months. I didn't think about him much, although what happened that day in August crossed my mind several times. Once, in a dream he came to me. He hovered above me and I could see his eyes very closely looking into my own, as I looked deeply into his. I wondered about that then, but still didn't give it much attention. Then one day in October, I was anxious and nervous and couldn't put my finger on why. I was scheduled to assist Patricia in class that night, and I can remember entering the teaching room, feeling apprehension. Some of the students were already there, hugging and saying their hellos.

Charles was one of the last ones to walk in. His demeanor is charismatic, and everyone noticed him. He went about saying hello and hugging those he knew in the class. When it came to me, it was as natural as day to hug him, and yet, I became unbearably shy when I did. I was afraid to speak to him, and feared he might speak to me. The very thought made me tremble. What was wrong with me? I felt like a shy little girl. When he complimented me on my haircut, I was surprised that he noticed. After a quick thank you, I took a seat. Wouldn't you know that the only seat left in the room was the one next to me? As fate would have it, that's where he sat. I could feel currents of energy flowing between us, and became uncomfortable when I realized that the others in the room were watching us, seemingly mesmerized. Even my mother appeared to be looking at us too. And all I could think was, "My God, what's going on here?"

After class I quickly made my escape and went home. I didn't understand what I was feeling. I recognized that I had felt drawn to Charles, but I wasn't ready to act on that feeling. If a relationship between us were meant to be, it would happen regardless of my action or inaction. I had been divorced and widowed and knew that if I were ever to marry again, it would be forever. I was willing to wait. My last thought before I went to sleep that night was that Mauricio might have sent this man to me.

Charles was not in my class the next morning, but several people asked me what had been going on. Apparently, they had seen sparks of energy moving between us and they were quite curious. I was shocked at this revelation. I didn't know what to say, so I just smiled. I couldn't lie and say there was nothing going on, even though I didn't know what was going on either! That day on the road, the day I first recognized Charles' eyes, my mother had also noticed white lights moving in and around our hearts, but didn't say anything to me at the time. It was only after Charles and I were together that she told me she had known that day that our two souls were meant to be together.

During the dinner break Charles and I ended up outside. As soon as he spoke to me, my shyness was gone. Charles is outgoing and has a strong personality. He was always talking or singing in or outside of class. But I could sense a quiet strength and gentle nature underneath, and I was at home in his energy. I found it easy to talk to this man. We talked about everything and we talked about nothing. It was as if two long lost friends had come together and picked up the conversation where they'd left off.

The rest of the week we talked a few more times, mostly during class breaks, but it was all very light and on the surface until the day his class ended. Charles had a break before his next class and asked if I would meet him later that day. I told him that I would. That afternoon we walked down to the Cherokee healing passage, in the woods. I can remember looking into his eyes and suddenly recognizing who he was! I knew those eyes. I had seen them before. They were the eyes I had seen in my dream in Vienna!

I was shocked. Charles was a married man. How could this be? This supposed love of mine, a married man? That was not supposed to be a part of it. But when Charles saw my eyes searching deeply into his own, it was as if he knew exactly what I was feeling and thinking, and he replied, "One day you won't look at me with those question-ing eyes, Kimberly." On some level, we already knew deep in our hearts that we were meant to be together, but we didn't know quite how it was going to happen. As we sat there quietly in each other's energy, we agreed that we wouldn't pursue a relationship until his life was more settled.

Charles had just retired from a thriving business career. For twen-ty-five years he had been the Tire King of Florida and, with an initial investment of less than five hundred dollars, had built one of the largest independent chains of tire stores in America, Tire Kingdom. Charles, or Chuck as he was known then, had gained a great deal of recognition for his wacky TV commercials featuring the Tire King and other assorted characters. When he sold his company to Michelin in 1989, he continued to run it as its Chief Executive Officer. Four years later, with Wall Street partners, he bought the company back with the intention of taking it public. Sometimes life doesn't turn out the way you expect it.

Charles had devoted his life to being a good father, a good hus-band, and a good businessman. It was his role in life, so he thought, and he played it very well for twenty-eight years. He lived his life for his family and his work, and he had everything life is supposed to offer: fame and fortune, beautiful children, a loyal and devoted wife, and a magnificent oceanfront estate on Jupiter Island. But on the inside he knew that something was missing. All of the material things that he possessed or could acquire failed to fill his belly.

At the age of seventeen, Charles had joined the Marines, and was soon shipped off to Vietnam. It was here that he lost his faith. He couldn't understand how an all-loving God could allow such suffer-ing to take place. Later, Charles would become agnostic. His inner knowing sensed that there was a higher power, a divine force that gave life to all things. He just didn't feel that the church or others had accurately identified just what that power was. Three events later occurred in his life that opened him up to the possibility that God did indeed exist.

The first of these occurred on the eve of a civil trial in Miami that his company was involved in. A competitor had sued his company in an attempt to put them out of business. It was a particularly difficult lawsuit with hundreds of depositions and questionable tactics by the plaintiff. It took nearly two years of preparation, and on the eve of trial, everyone was sure that Charles was headed for a nervous breakdown. That night, he awoke and was bathed in a blue cosmic light. As the light washed over him, he felt a peace and a calm, and he knew that he was truly in the presence of God. Everything would now be all right, he felt, which it was.

The second of these "events" was a book called *Many Lives, Many Masters* by Brian Weiss, given to him by a friend. The book was written by a psychiatrist whose patient, while under hypnosis, recounted over 80 past lives that held the clues to her current day illnesses. Much later, Charles would undergo past life regression at the Brian Weiss Institute, where he would also learn of his own past lives and their current meaning.

Some years later, Charles was invited to see the famous Filipino healer, Alex Orbito. Alex has the ability to reach into a person's body and take out diseased tissue and remove energy blocks. Literally. When Charles experienced his energy, and watched this man heal hundreds of people before his very eyes, it gave him hope that there was a God and he did indeed perform miracles.

But it was many years later that Charles was to have an experience that would change his life forever. It was a Sunday morning in October of 1995. As was his custom, every Sunday morning he would take a ride around his Jupiter Island property. The property was very large, almost nine acres stretching from the Atlantic Ocean to the Indian River, and Charles would ride around the property in a golf cart. He loved this place. It was paradise. He typically would ride down to the intra-coastal side of the property to check out the fish, like snook and snapper, and the wading birds that inhabited the waters here. He would then ride around other parts of the property to check out the flowers and butterflies, maybe stop and shoot some hoops, and then go over to the beach.

On this day, Charles wasn't doing particularly well. He was experiencing a public relations crisis in his business, and was shifting between feeling sorry for himself, and feeling angry at the injustice of it. It seemed like each time his company was poised to move up to the next level, something unforeseen would happen that would stop their progress. On the property were a number of giant banyan trees, hundreds of years old, with their twisted and majestic roots and branches, and their billowing leaves. That day, Charles was headed along the path from the river to the main house when he decided to stop under one of the trees and look up. As he looked up, he remembered reading that the Buddha received enlightenment under a banyan tree. He lifted his head and cried out, "Why God, why does this always happen to me?" Suddenly he felt a jolt of energy that made him quiver, and immediately out of his mouth came the answer, in a voice that was not his own, "because you have purpose Charles."

Charles thought that he had finally lost his mind. Each time he had a thought or asked a question, the answer would come without delay. "Who are you?" he asked. "You know who I am," the voice answered. "God, is that you?" "Yes, beloved," came the reply. What followed was a long dialogue between them. Charles experienced the gamut of emotion from jubilation and excitement to fear and anxiety, and he realized and knew that being human is not all that we truly are, but is a temporary condition we experience as eternal beings with immortal souls, who have chosen to project a part of themselves in human form to experience life on earth. He also learned in that particular moment to lighten up and stop taking things so seriously, that God was here and all was well.

God had come to Charles to let him know that he had a purpose in this life, and to ask him if he was willing to fulfill it. Three times God had asked him if he was willing, and each time Charles replied that he was unworthy and that God should find another. And God simply said, "No Charles, you are the one." Finally, he agreed and said, "Yes Lord, I will do it if you want me to. Thy will be done."

After this, Charles became very excited and ran to tell his wife and children who were in the house. But he then thought better of it. "Did that really happen?" he wondered. "Or am I just losing my mind?" Did he really understand what had just happened? Or what his purpose was to be? He really wasn't sure. At the beach later that afternoon, he once again he felt the surge of energy come into him. And again, the dialogue began. This time, in addition to the revelations, he was also experiencing visions, visions of a near future in which many would struggle. He had flashes of significant changes in the world, of Nostradamus, of Plato and Aristotle, of the Middle East, and of things that made little sense to him. And again God asked if he would do his will. And once more he resisted and then agreed.

Finally, at sunset, Charles was visited again. Only this time all anxiety had passed. He asked again, "Lord are you sure it's me you want? Isn't there another more suitable? After all, who am I?" And God replied, "Charles, you are the one I am asking." And Charles answered, "I love you Father, and I will do whatever you want me to do." And then it was over. Charles remembered how the Christ had asked three times for the burden to be taken from him too, and he knew in that moment that his life would never be the same. He still wasn't sure what his purpose was or how his life would change. But he trusted and knew that whatever God had in store for him, he would be okay.

In the following months Charles was magically led to the people and places that would enable him to gain a greater understanding of who he was and where he was going. He began to break free of his old restraints and duties, and he gave six months notice to his partners that he was leaving the company. One month later he was forced to resign, the day before he was scheduled to come to Delphi. His greater understanding and awareness had now led him to Delphi, and to me.

When we returned from the healing passage, Charles and I were feeling quiet and peaceful. We walked back to the school and sat down to meditate together. It was a most incredible experience. Our vision was one. The interaction of our spiritual selves was like an orchestra, and the universe was ours. Light swirled around us, above us and through us. We were intertwined with the light and it was as if our own spiritual lights were cosmically dancing together. The energy was so intense and so strong that it held us for hours. Time stood still. When we came back, we just looked at each other without speaking. We knew that our souls had just experienced our future together. Our souls had reconnected from a shared past, and our spiritual love and energy was united once again.

Charles left after class ended the next week. I expected he would return home, do what he had to do, and come back to me when we could be together, some time in the future. I was very comfortable with that, knowing I would have time to ease into the next chapter of my life. I was still a bit unsure about what to expect from another relationship and whether I could or should even try to recapture the kind of love I had with Mauricio. I should have known that just as each person is different, so too is the love, just as deep, but different. I trusted that whatever the universe would bring was right, and I was willing to let it unfold. The Universe has a way of giving us what we need, and not always what we expect.

It took Charles a lot of courage to leave a relationship after twenty-eight years. I had been divorced after five years, and widowed after only four. I remembered how difficult those endings were for me. I couldn't imagine how painful it was going to be for a family that had spent all of their lives together. So many families go through this crisis, and it is painful for each family member. Charles and I spent almost two years going through his divorce, and I felt his pain deeply. It is very difficult not to get pulled in emotionally and feel terrible for hurting the ones that you love, despite your good intentions.

Charles had to do what was right for him. He told me later that he knew this was his window of opportunity to fulfill the rest of his life's purpose. He knew that if he wasted this opportunity, his purpose for being on earth was no longer valid, and he would surely die. To him, it was a life and death decision. Still, at times the guilt became too much for him. Sometimes he thought he should return to his family. Sometimes I thought he should, too. There were plenty of things that might have broken us up, but every time it got shaky, something happened that made us recognize our purpose together. We persisted. We got married in August 1998, at our new home, with Patricia officiating.

The night before our wedding, I went outside and stood on the deck, feeling humble and very grateful for the opportunity to love again. Tomorrow would be the day I would dedicate myself to this love for the rest of my life. But before I did, in some odd way I felt that I had to say good-bye to Mauricio again. It had only been five years since his death and I too, am a loyal person. It wasn't easy for me to let go of the feelings for him that sometimes consumed me during the years I was alone. I sent my love out into the universe and called upon Mauricio's energy. The trees began to move and I saw their auras emanate their life force. Everything felt so alive, and the joy and brightness of it enveloped me. I felt a kinship with all life. I could hear crackles of electricity and I saw a few sparks. I knew Mauricio was there and that he was happy with me. I felt overwhelmed by love and I thought of my mother's vision. A year earlier Mauricio came to Patricia to say that I was okay and that he was now free to lift further. He had watched over me for these past years and it was time for all of us to move on. Patricia could see him struggling emotionally to let me go. It was difficult for him and he needed help. A huge angel with the most beautiful wings then appeared. The angel put her arms around Mauricio and as they began to lift, all my mother could think of was how beautiful Mauricio looked. His hair was white and long and his face was brilliant. He was magnificent in a way that he had never been here on earth. His presence was pure and angelic. He radiated light. Reading my mother's thoughts, Mauricio stopped and slowly turned back to look at her. "You look like this, too," he said. She was so moved, she began to cry. She understood that what he said applied to every one of us. After Mauricio's visit, my mother knew that I would be okay, and that life with Charles was truly my next step.

Our wedding day was bedlam. It was hot and humid, and our new driveway had not yet been poured. So the guests had to be delivered through the mud by a shuttle van. In typical fashion, I was late to my own wedding. In the true spirit of the occasion, I had insisted the hairdresser work his magic on all the other women in the wedding party, so it took some time before my hair was done. I hadn't forgotten about my friend the opera singer who'd had a vision of Charles during our dinner in Vienna. Back then I had joked with her, telling her I would fly her to America to sing at my wedding if her prediction came true. Well, there in the front row, awaiting her cue, sat Shake Kazajian, who sang Ave Maria for us.

Our wedding was a celebration of love in which everyone had a part. It was our intention to create such a feeling of love, harmony and unification that everyone there felt it. Charles and I wrote our own vows and, in front of everyone, Charles sang "Grow Old Along With Me," a song that John Lennon wrote for Yoko Ono. When I looked into his eyes I knew that this was the final love of my life, that we would indeed grow old together. I still get goose bumps when I think about the hugs Charles and I received from Marshall and Patrick right after the ceremony. And I still laugh when I remember how, a few years after Mauricio had died, the boys started asking me if I was ever going to get married again. I kept telling them then, "Oh, the man who is trying to find me is probably lost. McCaysville is a very hard place to find." Then, when we became engaged, the boys were very quick to pull me aside and ask, "Mommy, are you sure Charles is the man who was trying to find you? He doesn't look like the kind of man who would get lost."

In our new home, Charles and I built a healing sanctuary and filled it with our most sacred objects and our love. Initially I was a bit nostalgic for the sanctuary in the home where Mauricio and I lived. But I soon discovered that the room we created had the same power, and that through our intention, we could and did attract the higher energies of love, light, and healing for our work. Charles has his own healing power, and together we have brought through the quality and essence of our combined energy.

I admire his ability to stay focused. It reminds me of Mauricio's intense concentration. Charles' devotion to healing is very much like Mauricio's, and I was able to appreciate that he possessed some of the same qualities I admired so much. My friends and family wondered how Charles was going to measure up to Mauricio's memory. He didn't have to, and anyway, why would he want to? The love that Mauricio and I shared was one of a kind. But so is the love I share with Charles. We have created our own way of working together and as we adjusted to married life, our spiritual purpose unfolded. Our love is complementary and full of life's experience. And we work both individually and together, deepening our commitment everyday, to help those in need.

17

The animal is satisfied with the mediocrity of
necessity; and the Gods are content with their
splendors. But man cannot rest permanently
until he reaches some highest good. He is the
greatest of living beings because he is the most
discontented, because he feels most the
pressure of limitations. He alone is capable of
being seized by the devine for an ideal.

–Sri Aurobindo

SOMETIMES I WONDER why life has been so good to me.
When I remember all that I lived through since my very first trip
to Brasilia, all the things that I learned, felt and experienced, I
can't believe how incredibly lucky I am. My marriage to Charles
would not have been possible without my relationship with Mauricio.
I truly learned who I was from Mauricio, a man many considered a
master.

While putting together the material for this book, my relationship
with Mauricio reached yet another level. One special evening,
Marshall my Papa, channeled Mauricio so I could ask him some
unanswered questions about the past. Mauricio spoke to me through
Marshall. He answered my questions, but I soon realized in our session, that the questions didn't matter, and my reason for being there
was different than I thought. I was there to receive a healing.

Up until that moment, there were times that I denied or didn't feel
my own strength and I would rely on Mauricio, asking for his. I
always received it. But in the past year when I felt myself reaching out
to use a part of his strength instead of my own, I wasn't feeling him
as strongly as I had in the past. I didn't understand that he was drawing away, ever so slightly, until he told me so during the channeling.
Then it became clear to me. Mauricio's love would always be there to
help fulfill my work. But it was time for me to use my own strength,
my own energy, my own power, and not be dependent on him. Once
again, Mauricio taught me to grow and stretch into my own purpose.

I had always wanted to ask Mauricio if he was the one who sent Charles to me, but never had. His smile went piercing through me as he lit up. He told me yes, but that he was only a small part of it, that it was angelically ordained. He told me that Charles was my next step and that we would fulfill our purpose together. I began to cry as he told me to love Charles with all my heart. Waves of love were moving through me, energizing me, and I realized just how deeply I do love Charles, and I wanted to love him even more.

Mauricio had reached into my heart and removed yet another layer. He severed the last thread that held us to a dependent relationship. Our love is still and always will be strong, but the emotional dependency is gone. We share a love so deep and profound that it can never be changed or diminished by time or distance, but we can now work in a way that we never could before. We are fulfilling the terms of our spiritual contract together. My part of the contract is to continue his work here, and his part is to help me do so.

Now, I am free to love Mauricio unconditionally, but I no longer need to rely on him emotionally. He has freed me to love and to be loved by Charles. And I am free to pursue the next level on my path, as I am supposed to do. Without him, but never without his love.

Reference Text

Dyer, Dr. Wayne W. *Your Erroneous Zones.* Harper Perennial, reprinted by permission of Funk & Wagnall, 1976.

Dyer, Dr. Wayne W. *Real Magic: Creating Miracles in Everyday Life.* New York, Harper Paperbacks, A Division of HarperCollins Publishing, 1992: 75, 76-78.

Hayes, Patricia and Marshall Smith. *Extension of Life: Arthur Ford Speaks.* Roswell, Georgia, Dimensional Brotherhood Publishing House, 1986.

Lama Surya Das. *Awakening the Buddha Within.* New York, Broadway Books, 1997: 13.

Levine, Robert M. *The History of Brasil. The Greenwood Histories of the Modern Nations.* Frank W. Thackeray and John E. Findling, Series Editors. Westport, Connecticut, Greenwood Press, 1999: 124–126.

Shoumatoff, Alex. *The Capital of Hope.* New York: Coward, McCann & Geoghegan, Inc., 1980: 19.

Contact Us

For additional information about Delphi, please contact us:

Delphi University
P.O. Box 70
940 Old Silver Mine Road
McCaysville, GA 30555
706/492-2772
e-mail: registrar@delphi-center.com

Visit our Web site at www.delphi-center.com.

August 23, 1992

Dear Mauricio,

During your recent visit to Lily Dale I was fortunate enough to experience the Lights with you. Prior to that time I had decided due to personal problems...an abusive marriage, financial troubles, drug additions in my children, etc., that I did not wish to live any longer. My body, obeying the messages from my mind, was responding by developing kidney problems.

When I left for Lily Dale I was scheduled upon my return for x-rays. My doctor had discovered a firm mass of unidentifiable origin in the stomach area. When I saw you, I was in a great deal of physical pain. The next morning most of it was gone. By the time I returned home and had the x-rays there was no evidence of the mass at all.

I realize that I want to live now and my outlook is so much more positive. I didn't know if people tell you the wonderful things you do and how much you are appreciated! Thank you so very much for what you do. You and Kimberly are beautiful together...you exude caring and love. Thank you. Thank you. Thank you. I will never forget what you did for me.

Blessings,

Jill Carruthers

179

Special Thanks

I would like to acknowledge and thank the following people who continue to share Mauricio's gift of light with others through energization:

Ed Aguilar	RioRico, AZ
Julia Allen	Waite Hill, Ohio
Gloria Andreoli	Winter Springs, FL
Howard Batie	Chehalis, WA
Marian Bollinger	Kingsville, MD
Linda Bowman	Palmetto, FL
Stephen Carl	Centerville, OH
Sophie Cartier	Paris, France
Patrick Castellucci	Alexandria, VA
Sandy Castellucci	Alexandria, VA
Michiyo Chew	Prospect Heights, IL
Yvonne Christman	Bloomingdale, IL
Emmy Chetkin	Lily Dale, NY
Phillipe Coffin	Paris, France
Charles Curcio	McCaysville, GA
Leyan De Borga Hindman	Baltimore, MD
Jayma Delaney	Valley City, OH
Helen Descovich	Vienna, Austria
Deborah Echanis	Frankford, DE
Robert Ericsson	Lincolnwood, IL
April French	Stockbridge, ME
Ray Gage	McCaysville, GA
Jo Galloway	Waynesville, NC
Mary Goodley	New York, NY
Joni Gray	New London, NH
Ramona Hamill	Allentown, PA
Marie France Hankinson	Charleston, SC
Meg Hayworth	Saluda, SC

Sharon Hendershot	Freehold, NJ
Peter Howe	Greenfield, MA
Loretta Huinker	Yorktown, VA
Julia Jackson	Siver Springs, MD
Christie Jaffe	Greencastle, IN
Robin Kepner	Canandaigua, NY
Lynda Klaes	Bettles, AK
Joan Lohan	Hamilton, Bermuda
Nancy Lloyd	Greensboro, NC
Irene McCormack	Haverhill, MA
Elissa MacLachlan	Las Vegas, NV
Kymberly Manni	Okemos, MI
Lucrezia Mangione	Oxford, CT
Marc Mario	Rome, NY
Ruth Martin	Atlanta, GA
Beth McConnell	Missouri City, TX
James McShane	Lindsay, Ontario, Canada
Elizabeth McVoy	Montclair, NJ
Cullen McVoy	Montclair, NJ
Margo Murdock	Macon, GA
Pamela Neeley	Cameron, TX
Valerie O'Connor	West Melford, NJ
Tomothy O'Leary	Cambridge, MA
Carole O'Ryan	Ashville, NC
Donna Pappalardo	Eastchester, NY
Antonio Pasin	Chicago, IL
Suban Potijinda	Virginia Beach, VA
Judy Potter	McCaysville, GA
Georgia Putnam	Charlotte, NC
Marcy Prisco	Wayne, NJ
Susan Raef	Chicago, Ill
Teresa Riccio	Salisbury, MD
Lynn Rice	Harwich, MA
Erin Riley	Culver City, CA
Judith Rovin	Mandeville, LA
Rose Sangregoria	Calgary, Alberta
Cherie Santasiero	Hamburg, NY
Katharine Scrimgeour	Harbor Island, Bahamas
Lydia Serra	Montreal, Ontario, Canada
Tina Marie Shipp	Winston-Salem, NC

Dawn Sigurdson	Blackfalls, Alberta, Canada
Lydia Silva	Watervliet, NY
Cynthia Stajos	Haslett, MI
Sharon Strait	Stuart, FL
Paula Strong	Litchfield, CN
Lorraine Taber	Redfield, NY
Karen Thomson	Kennessaw, GA
Floriana Venetico	Savannah, GA
Sue Warm	Naples, FL
Joan Wash	Mechanicsville, VA
Nora Walsh	Antonio, TX
Nancy Welsh	Irwin, PA
Bernice White	Hamilton, Bermuda
Kay Wilson	Fairbanks, AK

Glossary

Akashic Records
The record of an individual's past, present, and future lives and experiences on the physical and astral planes. It is said that the Akashic records are stored in the left ventricle of the heart. Gifted individuals have the ability to access these records.

Aura
Auras are the energy fields that surround the physical body. They are composed of the subtle bodies and the energy emanations of the physical body, which change according to the person's mood and environment. Some people can read these fields and from them discern problems or issues in that person's life.

Chakras
Chakra is a Sanskrit word meaning "wheel." The charkas are energy centers, the distributors of life force energy to the physical body. There are seven primary charkas and numerous secondary ones, arranged down the middle of the body and in the extremities, starting above the head and extending below the feet.

Dis-ease (Disease)
Western medicine's view of illness/disease is a cause and effect relationship. Although it can't explain why a child is born with diabetes or leukemia, or why someone who has never smoked has contracted lung cancer, it espouses heredity or genetic factors as a physical cause of illness.

In spiritual belief one creates an illness as a way to learn a lesson in order to experience spiritual growth in this lifetime. This interpretation relies on the belief that everything we see and experience in the world around us is a reflection of how we feel about ourselves and our relationship to the world. Dis-ease is the opposite of ease. It means that something is out of order or out of balance.

Ectoplasm
Is accumulated life force energy, sometimes referred to as prana,

which is concentrated through he focus of mediums to assist the healing process. Ectoplasm can also be used as a natural anesthesia.

Energization
Is Mauricio's process, where the higher energies of light are evoked to bring healing and awaken ones spiritual abilities. Energization brings through a quality of spiritual substance that energizes the physical, emotional, mental, and spiritual bodies. During energization, one could have a mystical experience leaving them in an altered state for some time.

Etheric Body
The etheric body is an energy field that closely surrounds, envelopes, and animates the physical body. It is the energy 'double' of the physical body. It is the etheric body that supplies vital life force energy to the physical body. When Mauricio brought the lights, they emanated from his etheric body, not from his physical body.

Kundalini
The Kundalini, located at the base of the spine, is the vital life force that flows through all physical life. The word kundalini means 'snake', and is the descriptive name given to the flow of spiritual energy through the chakras. Mauricio used the Kundalini breath to bring healing energy during an energization.

Medium
People who have a natural gift or who have been trained to access their gifts to bring psychic and spiritual information and energy into physical reality,

Spirit
The invisible force that moves behind and through all things. Spirit can be described as pure energy that comes from God from which all creation is formed.

Stigmata
The stigmata is a condition where one displays the wounds of the crucifixion of Jesus. Mauricio exhibited a form of stigmata, perfect round marks over his chakras, on the palms of his hands, and in the shape of the cross over his heart. There were only three reasons the lights ever entered Mauricio's physical body: to energize and communicate with him, to humble him, or to prepare him to perform a healing on a very sick person. When the lights entered his body under those circumstances, they entered through his stigmata.